Campus Crusade for Christ Library

T4-AHE-232

STUDIES IN MINISTRY AND WORSHIP

EDITOR: PROFESSOR G. W. H. LAMPE

WHAT IS CHRISTIAN GIVING?

What is Christian Giving?

BRIAN RICE

SCM PRESS LTD
56 BLOOMSBURY STREET
LONDON

First published 1958

© SCM PRESS LTD 1958

Printed in Great Britain by
The Camelot Press Ltd., London and Southampton

Campus Crusade for Christ Library

BV
772
R495
1958

CONTENTS

Foreword by the Right Reverend Richard S. Emrich, Bishop of Michigan   7

INTRODUCTION   9

THE AMERICAN SCENE   13

CHRISTIAN GIVING IN AMERICA   20
  The National Council of the Churches of Christ   21
  The National Council of the Episcopal Church   27
  Professional Fund-Raising   29
  The Diocese and Christian Giving   32
  The Diocese of Chicago   33
  The Diocese of Michigan   38
  Among Parishes and Missions   51

THE ENGLISH SCENE   54
  What is Tithing?   58
  What is the Christian Standard of Giving?   59
  Why do People decide to Tithe?   60
  Do People grow in grace through Tithing?   61
  How to decide what is a Grateful Share   64
  How do People get started on Tithing?   64
  People ask these Questions about Tithing   66
  Is it Christian to teach Abstract Giving?   67
  What about Bazaars and Sales of Work?   68
  Is Christian Giving an Act of Worship?   69
  What does the Bible Teach about Christian Giving? 70

THE WAY AHEAD   75
  Will it work here?   75
  Practical Suggestions   79

5

14037

APPENDIX   83
    I   A Critique of Professional Fund-raising   83
    II The Conduct of the Every Member Canvass   87
    III The Covenant Scheme   95

TO

MY THEOLOGICAL TEACHERS

ALDEN D. KELLEY

AND

OLIVER S. TOMKINS

FOREWORD

BY THE BISHOP OF MICHIGAN

Dear Mr Rice,

I am happy to write this Foreword and do so on the basis of the letter I wrote you recently.

I read your discussion with great interest and profit. It contains much valuable material. In a year you could not see the whole of Church life in the States, but you have set down your impressions with accuracy and charity. Christian Giving is of vital concern to our whole Anglican Communion and we are glad for you to spread details of experiments in America.

You are wise not to tell a big American success story. This would alienate English readers and it is good that your discussion is closely related to parish life in England. Michigan is a rich area—the highest wages in the world. The State of Maine is more like the English village scene and there is no such 'success' story there. We should teach Modern Tithing because it is right, serious and responsible, not because it is successful. It springs from gratitude to God and is a means of grace that leads us closer to Him. I am glad that you emphasize that Giving is Christian and not just an American phenomenon. Stewardship applies to all God's children and should be taught everywhere. A parish does not require a professional firm to teach it Stewardship and Tithing. There is a place for professional fund-raisers in conducting capital drives like the one in Michigan because they alone have the necessary skill and experience. At the same time no vicar need wait for a capital campaign before leading his congregation in Tithing.

When one begins to teach Tithing, probably little will happen.

The important thing is that it is true and in the right direction. Even in the long haul we reach only partial success. But whatever its results, Christian Giving springs from the heart of the Faith and goes with full seriousness to the heart of the believer. It centres round theology, personal religion and worship.

I rejoice that so much attention is being given to Christian Giving. It concerns all of us. If this discussion helps to awaken parish clergy and lay leaders into thinking out and applying Christian Giving, what you have written will abide and be of the greatest value.

I pray that this may be God's will.

Richard S. Emrich
BISHOP OF MICHIGAN

Lambeth,
August 1958

INTRODUCTION

THIS monograph is the work not of an expert but of an eye-witness. Its purpose is to discuss Christian Giving, with reference to the Protestant Episcopal Church in America. These experiences are set down deliberately in the form of a discussion. It is not possible to offer a handbook on Christian Giving with easy applications and slick answers. Indeed if we had time to listen to ourselves talking about money, we would hear a babel of voices. Most writers on evangelism and parish action to-day mention the low standard of Christian Giving in England and advocate further thought on this subject. These suggestions are both proper and widespread, but many indicate the surprising expectation that congregations will start giving without being trained to give. The view taken in this discussion is that the outstanding problem in so many parishes is *not* that people do not give but that they are not *trained* to give. And in this era of personal and national prosperity, thousands of good Christians are *deeply concerned* with the question, 'What is the right standard of giving to the Church?'

The beginning of wisdom lies in trying to ask the right questions. Most of this material has resulted from asking and listening on both sides of the Atlantic for several years, and the actual experiences of many people are preferred to the theories of an individual.

I arrived in New York in September, 1955. The World Council of Churches had awarded me a scholarship and my destination was Seabury-Western Theological Seminary, Evanston, Illinois. But this was hardly the beginning. I had met several American clergy while studying in Jerusalem the previous year and their approach to parish life had impressed me. Thus when I had the opportunity to apply to the British Council of Churches, I asked for consideration for a place in a seminary of the Protestant Episcopal Church.

The scope of the scholarship was two-fold: to continue theological studies and to learn from the American Church. This allowed me a delightful year in Evanston and I am grateful to the Dean, Faculty and fellow-students for their friendship and affection. The National Council of the Episcopal Church provided a generous allowance and enabled me to visit parishes and conferences in several parts of the States. Fortunately my rooms were above the National Council's Unit of Research which was then housed at Seabury-Western, and the latest information and strategy were always available.

These details may seem tedious, but they are set down not only in gratitude but as the indispensable basis of learning. The way to learn from another Church is to stay for a long time and move around freely. I did both; and saw and wrote down things which any guest from the Church of England would have noted. Thus the discussion is not original. It is a product of many minds and situations on both sides of the Atlantic.

I had nearly a year's warning before leaving England. This allowed ample time for preparation, especially in finding out what were the main areas of concern among parish priests. Advice from several levels convinced me that finance was a great problem. The religious press contains many appeals for money. At the time of writing the *Church Times* contains details of new appeals totalling over £464,000; and this is true most weeks. If we could solve the financial situation we might receive fresh impetus and insight into other spiritual problems. This concerned me because most of my relatives are in the business world and so I have grown up in surroundings where the practical application of the Christian Faith has been uppermost. I set out for America persuaded that we were 'ahead' in theology and that the Episcopal Church was 'ahead' in practical application and 'know-how'.

The discussion indicates how living as an Episcopalian caused me to alter and correct opinions widespread in England. One of the most enduring results of the visit has been the realization that many American evangelistic methods originated in England and that increasing space in the libraries of English clergy and theological students is given to works by American theologians. It is sad to discover that little is actually known in England about the American Church apart from its impressive statistics. Yet frequently when evangelism is discussed at chapter meetings and other conferences on a local level, there are vague references to the American scene. This lack of knowledge is tragic when it concerns problems which the Americans have partially solved or made great progress in, but which baffle and beat parish priests in England. Christian Giving is one of these problems.

It is a great honour that Bishop Emrich has read the manuscript and written the Foreword. What I have learnt about Christian Giving from the Diocese of Michigan is evident throughout the discussion. I am grateful to the Bishop for his kindly interest and to the Department of Promotion for permission to quote from diocesan publications. I am also grateful to a splendid team of friends—Mrs L. Hudson, Valerie Dyke, Brenda Mealing, Pat Wise, Cynthia and Roger Berwick—for help in assembling this material. Christian Giving with reference to the American Church was raised first in an article in *Theology* for September, 1957. I received many enquiries and encouraging letters, which taught me a great deal. I am especially grateful to a German theologian who sat next to a lonely English student on a New York train. I do not remember his name but I think of his wisdom every time I think of America. 'Young man,' he said, 'if you want to learn anything from the Church here, make a note of all you see and write it in question form—what is this for? why don't they do this? and so on. This is the way to penetrate the American scene. You won't find all the answers but you will grasp what is going on.'

What follows is an attempt to work out this wisdom. There are three stages in the discussion because there are three stages in any appreciation of the American scene:

(i) The Church has considerable financial resources at its disposal.
(ii) How does the Church raise its resources?
(iii) Why do Christians give so much?

These stages are more of a spiral than a straight line or a neat pattern. The evidence which illustrates them is frequently not characteristic of every American parish and diocese. It is offered in the desire to share some of the lessons which the American Church can teach, particularly with regard to the motives and application of Christian Giving. I should wish to withdraw any remarks in which I have misrepresented the American scene, or which are not written with charity. I use the expression 'American Church' to cover all Churches and all parts of the States. Christian Giving is not confined to one denomination or area; it is necessary to allow descriptions the widest application. I have used generally the nomenclature of the Episcopal Church and the Church of England; I imagine that non-Anglican readers will find no difficulty in making the necessary minor adjustments.

THE AMERICAN SCENE

No one could be in New York long without seeing the power of the American Church. I spent the first week-end with the minister of a down-town church in an industrial centre just outside New York. The 'Church plant' cost 1,000,000 dollars[1] and into it for morning service came nearly 1,000 people. Afterwards I waited in the clergy office and watched the collection being counted. It was £900—the weekly average! The English equivalent would be, perhaps, a working-class parish in which each worshipper gave 7s. 6d. weekly. I have mentioned this down-town church several times because it was my first experience of the American scene.

To get some idea of a down-town parish I asked about its main problems in evangelism. 'Problem number one,' said the minister, 'is finding escorts for week-night activities. This is a tough area and unless we provide escorts there is serious danger of folk being molested or beaten up.' Sometimes I endorse this statement by mentioning that on Christmas Eve I went to the aid of a woman and ran for the police in a second incident—all within five minutes of leaving Midnight Communion. This is sufficient indication of the area round one particular church. It is not characteristic of America as a whole, but it does begin to focus on Christian Giving. Here is a workers' church averaging a pound a person at a time when the national average wage was £27 weekly.

The effect of this congregation was tremendous. They had been trained to give and so their church had proper resources. There were twenty-two full-time paid workers. Only three were clergy. Imagine the striking power! The other nineteen workers included

[1] One dollar equals approximately seven shillings. The present exchange rate is £1 = $2.80.

parish secretaries, directors of religious education, youth officers, church business manager, caterer, publicity officer and so on: and these were assisted by part-time and voluntary workers. After the morning service lunch was provided for about 200 who remained for the adult instruction class which followed. The literature for the course was excellent and classes were tape-recorded so that absentees could hear it the following night.

This is Sunday in one American congregation. It may not be typical of the entire country, even where the Church is well established. Certainly it would be difficult or impossible to build up such a programme elsewhere. The American scene differs from England in so many respects that some of their methods will not apply here. But none of these considerations concern the main point: that where a congregation is being taught to give, the parish church will be developing the proper natural resources with which to spread the Gospel. Where clergy and people have not trained themselves to give, it is well nigh impossible to support the Church beyond the parish or to spread the Gospel resourcefully within it. The implication of this is not that we should raise money in order to promote American techniques, but that congregations should be taught to give so that the Church's work may go forward as our English scene requires. In my home parish it was noted recently that less was being given annually to missionary work now than at any time in the 1930's. It is this backward trend that training in Christian Giving can correct.

The story of one American parish is perhaps not destined to stir the imaginations of many. But there are other ways in which the resources of the American Church are immediately obvious to the visitor. These instances are given with a word of caution. One Episcopal criticism on my remarks on Christian Giving in America in *Theology* was that I gave the impression that the features described were more widespread than is in fact the case. This correction is proper. It is to the American Church that we may look for guidance in Christian Giving and fund-raising; yet they are themselves but pioneers in a field which we have scarcely

14

begun to explore. It is true that 'stewardship' plays a great part in American Church life, but the average church member and minister sees stewardship mainly in terms of raising money for church work. Thus the American Church has far to go in its own attitude to Christian Giving. Few of us, for example, would enthuse over a recent conference in Washington which rejoiced in a pamphlet, written by one cleric present, bearing the electrifying title: 'Money is God in Action.' But we in England would do well to follow the American lead so that we may share their success and failures, and thus grow in something which concerns our whole Anglican Communion so much.

One difference between English and American religious magazines is that those here often contain frantic appeals for money whilst their American counterparts are full of record budgets. From these record budgets flow record activity—although this is equally true the other way round. Record activity likewise develops into a record budget. One instance of this is the strength of the American theological seminaries. Most of those in the Episcopal Church are older than those in England but they are in splendid condition and well-staffed. At my American seminary we had 18 staff for 90 students; whereas in England this figure is usually 4-5 staff for 40-50 students.[1] A major reason for this difference is that American seminaries are more obviously the concern of the whole Church.[2] A glance at almost any American religious paper will reveal this. Here is an example of a large announcement, which appears in varying forms in every issue of the *Living Church* and occupies a full half-page 'SEMINARIES REPORT TO THE CHURCH—WITH THANKS. Parish Offerings for Theological Education Sunday in 1956 exceeded those of 1955 by nearly fifty thousand dollars, reaching a total of $474,067 (about

[1] It should however be remembered that a detailed comparison would need to take into account the question of how many of the American staff are part-time, and what additional part-time help the average English college can call on.

[2] In this respect, the Episcopal Church is more comparable to, say, the Church of Scotland or the Methodist Church in England.

£170,000) from 5,008 parishes. While these offerings go to support the current operations of the seminaries, they are in a real sense capital investments, safeguarding the supply and training of the Church's future leadership. The 1957 offering is in the making; every parish in the Church has an important interest in the result.' A list of Episcopal seminaries was given beneath.

It is true that there is no American equivalent of CACTM[1] to assist candidates, but the needs of the seminaries are brought home to every church member. And when people understand, then they give. The General Theological Seminary, which is the oldest and largest of the Episcopal Church, has recently announced plans for a major campaign that will make possible a greatly-needed expansion, especially of its already overcrowded library facilities. The target is set at three and a half million dollars and I have little doubt that they will reach it probably before this gets into print. When people understand, they give.

No one can go far in the United States without seeing church publicity. Most clergy realize that contact must precede conversion. When I have mentioned this in England, such a view is criticized frequently as 'unsound' or 'unspiritual'. But surely there is a place for church publicity among the essentials for envangelism in the 20th century. Last year one Sunday paper offered the Church Enquiry Centre advertisement space at £189 10s. per insertion and over 36,000 people have applied for courses of instruction. This is obviously a most successful way of evangelism but how rarely can the Church of England provide the money to reach these people. Recently I attended a men's meeting addressed by a representative of the Church Commissioners, Church Assembly, and a Diocesan Conference. During the discussion I enquired if these bodies had any public relations officer and what was done about publicity. The answer was amazing: 'If anyone wants to know anything, he can phone the Church Information

---

[1] The Central Advisory Council for the Training of the Ministry does disburse from Central Church sources large sums for theological training.

Board.' Presumably this is the best that can be done without sufficient money, and with the sort of outlook lack of money produces.

In the United States it is difficult to do anything without en-
countering the Church. The Church spreads by using every
modern resource—advertising in the press, in the buses, on the
stations, and of course, by training its clergy and lay-folk. There
are two wonderful family posters spread over the States at present.
Both show family groups. One says, 'Give them a faith to live by,'
and the other 'Worship with them each week.' On street corners
surrounding most Episcopal churches are bright permanent signs
stating, 'The Episcopal Church welcomes you'; and giving directions beneath.

Where the Church is teaching its members Christian Giving,
funds will be available for church building. In 1956 a record high
in church construction was reported by the Departments of Com-
merce and Labour in Washington, D.C. The $773,000,000 (about
£275 million) was $39 million more than the previous record estab-
lished in 1955. Government experts have predicted that the 1957
total will have exceeded $875 million. It is a wonderful inspiration
to visit churches in all sections of society which can claim that
parish building matches parish spirit. And it is tragedy when
English Bishops have to write: 'Money has had to be borrowed
from the Bank, but it is a matter of importance that the overdraft
obtained should be reduced as quickly as possible. It is, therefore,
the case that the Diocese will not feel able to embark upon capital
expenditure on new buildings in the immediate future unless the
whole or at least a very substantial proportion of the cost can be
found immediately either by a transferred war damage payment or
by local resources such as parish building funds and the like. This
will be disappointing news for parishes which were anticipating or
hopeful of considerable Diocesan assistance with such projects as
the building of new halls, but it is a decision which will, I am afraid,
have to be accepted with patience and resignation, as obviously we
cannot commit ourselves to expenditure which we have not the
funds to meet.'

'Are we paying our clergy enough?' This is the title of a report by the Chairman of the Episcopal Church's Joint Commission to Study Pension Plans and Clerical Salaries. The Episcopal Church is not paying its clergy enough. There is great concern in the U.S.A. that since 1939 the cost of living has gone up 97%, but the average of clergy stipends has gone up only 83%. In England, my own stipend is £300 (the Diocesan scale) plus unfurnished accommodation and Whitsuntide offering. In 1939 the figure would have been £200, and the cost of living has since risen by 161%. Since the last adjustment of this stipend, the national wage average has risen 26% according to the Ministry of Labour. I suppose that only experience will reveal the effect of clerical poverty on the life of the whole Church, just as only Christian Giving will be able to remedy it.

In these few paragraphs some indication has been given of how some of the resources of the American Church will manifest themselves to any visitor from the Church of England. Comparisons are inevitable, but they will solve very little. What they seem to suggest is that one reason why so many people attend worship in the States is because the Church is developing all its resources to bring folk into the Family of God. And if these ways of using resources do not commend themselves to English readers, it is not difficult to think of other spheres where the spread of the Gospel cannot go forward because of financial difficulty. It is the point behind the American evidence which is crucial—that the American Church has money to use because it has discovered how to raise it. It is not difficult to disagree with some ways in which the money is used, but this should not obscure the point behind the evidence.

There are spheres in which the American Church can learn from the Church in England. Indeed it is surprising to discover how many of their methods are of English origin. But the sphere of Christian Giving is not in this category. The idea that the American Church 'knows all the answers' soon puts English backs up. It is not my intention to convey such an impression because such an estimate would be utterly false. I moved about in the States long enough to see for myself what the Rector of Trinity Parish, New York, meant when he said: 'It is customary for all of us to lay the blame for public indifference to religion at the door of the secularism and materialism of our age. It is my personal opinion that neither of these does us as much harm as does the constant parade of trivialities which the typical church programme offers to the public.' But the sphere of Christian Giving is not in this category.

It may seem inconsistent to mention power and triviality at the same time. But I am trying to set down some varying characteristics of the American scene so that the discussion may be followed with some appreciation of the context in which Christian Giving is worked out. This section has contained some indication of the more obvious resources of the American Church and some comparison with the English scene. This is part of the immediate reaction of any visitor. I cannot recall how long it took me to conclude that the American Church has powerful resources, but it is an instantaneous and compelling fact. These experiments in Giving in America must not be dismissed as 'American'—as they are by some, mainly those who have never been across the Atlantic—but must be considered as Christian and shared in love.

CHRISTIAN GIVING IN AMERICA

How does the American Church raise money? There are many successful experiments but no established formula. There is no such thing as 'American Giving' and I was properly corrected when using this expression. But the fact remains that Americans do give generously and many of them know why they are giving. However this is in response to no one 'system' and some parts of the States are very backward in Christian Giving. Finance is still a problem to the Church in America, but not a problem without hope or solution. In 1957 about $3,425,000,000 was given by Americans for religious purposes. This figure is 9% above the 1956 level. Religious construction during 1957 was valued at $870,000,000. Total philanthropic giving rose 4% from 1956 to 1957.[1]

This section describes and discusses Christian Giving in America. The scene is examined at all levels—national, diocesan, parochial and new mission churches—and from this emerge some of the principles of Christian Giving. The centres of concentration are the principles rather than the statistics because the principles are universal and therefore applicable in England. To establish the statistical basis for these principles I visited the Joint Department of Stewardship and Benevolence of the National Council of Churches. This Department has statistics of Giving by major denominations from 1929 until the present day, tabulated by its Bureau of Research and Survey. It would be tedious to reproduce all the charts and tables at my disposal; accordingly the statistics are restricted and attention focussed on methods and applications. Facts and figures quoted are usually the latest available: most have been revised since I left in 1956 and some are correct to the end of 1957.

[1] These figures are supplied by the American Associations of Fund-Raising Counsel.

The Joint Department of Stewardship and Benevolence heads its compilations 'Contributions from *Living* Donors'. Certainly the Church Commissioners have very limited capital under this heading. Americans are now giving more than three billion[1] dollars annually for the work of the Church. Last year the 41 denominations and churches reporting to the Joint Department showed a 10·1% gain (on previous year) in contributions to congregational expenses and an 8·2% gain in financing work beyond the local church. The American Association of Fund Raising Counsel announced that the assets of religious organizations showed an increase of more than $600 million in 1956 over the previous year. The 1955 table for denominations reporting their per capita gifts for that year for all purposes places the Wesleyan Methodists[2] first with $177 followed by the Seventh-day Adventists with $174. The Episcopal Church was twenty-second with $54.

Before these tremendous resources overwhelm English readers (as they overwhelmed me!), the American scene must be taken apart and examined from different angles. Such an analysis is somewhat artificial, but the different aspects, when pieced together, will provide a comprehensive and accurate picture of Christian Giving with reference to the American Church.

THE NATIONAL COUNCIL OF THE CHURCHES OF CHRIST

It is difficult to write on one aspect of the vast American Church without reference to other features. As I wrote in *Theology*, 'I focus here on finance, but involved is the total application of Christian stewardship, in which the American Church can teach us a great deal (and *vice versa*)'. Christian Giving cannot be separated from Christian living, nor discussed in isolation. Perhaps the outstanding characteristic of American church life is the emphasis on increased activity by lay folk, chiefly centred on a vigorous conception of stewardship and parish education. That this is so

[1] In the U.S. 'one billion' means 1,000 million; and this is the usage I am following in this book.

[2] The Wesleyan Methodists are a tiny 'sect group', not to be confused with the very large Methodist Church.

widespread is now due largely to the co-ordinating work of the National Council of the Churches of Christ in the United States of America.[1] This Council is divided into well-run departments, which help to co-ordinate and share the work of the member churches.

Thus the Council is responsible for publicizing experiments and advice in the sphere of Christian Giving. The Joint Department of Stewardship and Benevolence, in connection with the Department for Evangelism, sponsor most of the publications and guidance. The literature is excellent and most of it carries the definition of Christian Stewardship—'Christian Stewardship is the practice of systematic and proportionate giving of time, abilities, and material possessions, based on the conviction that these are a trust from God, to be used in His service for the benefit of all mankind in grateful acknowledgment of Christ's redeeming love.' The Department is well aware that dull and dowdy publications hinder the spread of the Gospel and so the quality of the literature is exceptional. It includes instructive pamphlets on Christian Giving for young and old, information on experiments, grace-cards for table, 'do-it-yourself' kits for parish posters, paper table mats and other attractive productions.

These centre round a movement almost unknown in this country—the Every Member Canvass. As American clergy tell their people, 'The accomplishments of your church in the coming year will depend, to a very large degree, on the kind of financial base you provide for its programs. A great deal of practical experience has shown that the most effective way to do this task is through an Every Member Canvass.' This takes place each autumn in many churches. The aim of the canvass is to bring the financial responsibility of the church to every individual member, as well as to certain friends in the community who are not affiliated to any other church. Another purpose is to get as many persons as

---

[1] The 'opposite number' of the British Council of Churches, but very much larger and more substantially supported. Certain large and active Churches are however not members of the National Council of Churches, notably the Southern Baptists and some of the Lutheran bodies.

possible to participate in the work. Experience shows that the success of canvassing for church funds depends on the degree to which the greatest possible number of people really understand the proposed programme.[1]

The first step towards a successful Every Member Canvass is an understanding of the theological basis of Christian Stewardship. The basis of Christian Stewardship is gratitude for God's greatest gift to us, the life, death, and resurrection of Jesus Christ. In him we see the supreme example of giving, and nothing in the life of his followers is more uniquely characteristic than giving for the good of others. This is a sound spiritual basis, though an English observer may feel that some American churches think of evangelism almost primarily in terms of efficient fund-raising and of Christian witness as confined to making regular donations. It is naturally difficult to document this impression. The sort of evidence I absorbed is reflected in a 'Top sayings of the month' (from popular preachers) item in a prominent church publication —'The Church that quits asking for money is dead.'

Two charts from the Joint Department of Stewardship and Benevolence are included in the Appendix. There is no doubt that Americans delight in and excel at 'know-how', and these charts contain valuable considerations for any parish contemplating its own programme for fund-raising. The Every Member Canvass seems to be the most widespread and proven of American methods and does *not* require outside direction.

The theme for the 1956-7 materials was 'Thy love I share'. This was on all literature, letter-headings, envelopes and so on, usually with the call 'GIVE to your Church'. The 1957-8 Canvass poster carries the ancient Christian symbols of the loaves and the fishes. This is an excellent choice, for it reminds us that God's gift to us is not something made from nothing—but something very great made from our modest human means. Thus Christians are reminded that God still asks for our modest gifts, our free giving

[1] The procedure of the Every Member Canvass is more fully described in the Appendix, pp. 87-95.

in proportion to our ability to give. In support of this poster are film strips, comic strips, canvass manuals and many other items. All these materials include instructions on how to use them effectively or on how to train others to use them effectively. It is suggested that the proposed budget face the following require-ments: our world mission; our pastoral ministry; our worship and service; our Christian education; our Church home. The items are set out over the words, 'For the coming year our Church has approved a programme to help to build Christ's Kingdom at home and abroad. To bring it into action, our Church must have . . . dollars. What our Church does for Christ . . . depends on what you and I give.'

Thousands of American church folk are catching on to this. 'What our Church does for Christ . . . depends on what you and I give.' They are *trained* to visit homes in the parishes to present the parish budget; they see plays and film-strips on how to en-courage others to support the work of the Church; they are shown the popular objections to fund-raising and given tested means to overcome them. The Diocese of Milwaukee, for example, has just developed three dialogues illustrating particular features of canvass calls to help train canvass workers. To some English readers these methods may sound too vast and streamlined. And the answer—if there is an answer—is that to-day the job of the Church in England is both big and urgent, and that it cannot be done without using our financial resources efficiently.

Other readers may feel, 'It all seems rather unspiritual!' But consider a new approach to financing that has been tried out by more than a thousand American churches, large *and small*, of various denominations. A group of churches in a New England town is typical. In 1955 their clergy were worried. Plans had been made for great things at home and abroad; but they could not go forward because all available funds had already been assigned. Now all that has been changed. In 1956 the treasuries were more than 60% fuller than the previous year. More Sunday school equip-ment and new hymnals have been purchased. Nearly all clergy salaries were increased and secretarial aid added. Help for missions was greatly increased and all the churches reported new vision and confidence. Church support had ceased to be a burden.

How did all this come about? The answer is to be found in the United Church Canvass. It combines deep Christian concern with the best methods of fund-raising and meets one of the most urgent needs of the Churches—getting alongside and working together. The United Canvass has strengthened many American churches in every way—spiritually, in fellowship, in love for all the life of the church, as well as financially.

This is how it worked out in one small town church which reported: 'Our church has had financial troubles for years. Our Sunday school room was entirely too small. We needed new equipment. Our pastor was only here part-time. But there were so few of us and we thought we could not afford to give more . . . we followed instructions and now we can hardly believe what has happened. People who have not yet joined the church gave more than our entire membership gave last year. And several of them have started to come to services. Now we have got the new equipment and also a full-time pastor. The religious education wing of the church is now being built. . . .'

How did they do it? The first step is to make a list of the people who will be asked to give ('pledge' is the American expression). Some churches simply present their programme and budget to their members. But there are many others who would feel honoured to have a share in carrying on the work of the church. And still others, such as parents of children who attend Sunday school, who owe a definite responsibility to the church. Children, too, should be trained in the privilege of giving to the church. Too many of them never advance beyond giving pennies at Sunday school. The spiritual value of Christian Giving, whether by children or adults, is significant. Worship is essentially self-giving, and, in a real sense, 'Your money is you'.

People never give generously simply to a 'good cause'. This—or the implication of it—is usually not grasped in England. *People give, not as they are able, but as they understand.* And those who need to realize this most of all are the clergy. A challenging programme must be presented to people. It must make some appeal to their imagination. They must be able to take some Christian pride in helping to support it. Some churches simply ignore this important consideration. When the responsible persons plan for the new year, their first—and perhaps only—question is: 'What did we do last year?' They forget that the need for Christian service is constantly growing and that no Christian church can stand still.

The climax of the whole canvass programme comes on Stewardship Sunday. There is a great variety in current practice. Giving cards are mailed to prospective givers. This is easy, but it is not very effective in providing funds for the church or blessings for the givers. In other churches, giving cards are distributed after a fine stewardship sermon. This plan certainly reaches those present. But judged by the record, the Every Member Canvass, by personal solicitation of Christian Giving in the homes, is without equal as a plan of church financing. It requires the enlistment of a large number of canvassers, and they *must* be well trained. The training of inexperienced people to do effective canvassing is a lot easier in America now than it used to be, thanks to recently developed teaching aids. This will be a top priority in England if we are to experiment with effective fund-raising. A lot of work is called for, but, as the Americans say, worth-while things seldom come in bargain packages!

The most appropriate conclusion for this section on the National Council of Churches is an extract from a report by the Director of the (Episcopal) Department of Promotion. He was reporting on his Australian trip, made late in 1957 at the invitation of the Australian Church's newly-created National Council for Promotion. The Director reported, 'I believe, from my limited observance, that Australia is *the* branch of the Anglican Communion to watch in the immediate future . . . the Church of England in Australia looks very much to the United States for help and guidance!' and he added that since its dioceses have no national organization comparable to the National Council, its current promotion effort is the first thing the Church has done on a national scale. The Director advised the Australian churches in four areas of this programme: (1) spreading the church's conception of promotion as 'A twentieth-century missionary force, not a high-powered sales technique limited to fund-raising'; (2) informing the Australians that the 'meaning of Stewardship is not synonymous with what one puts in the alms basin'; (3) reassuring the sceptics that the Every Member Canvass has a 'spiritual impact' in awakening laymen to their responsibilities; and (4) guiding them in the use of newspapers and TV.

Here is the American Church sharing its experiments and insights at the invitation of another branch of our Anglican Communion. If they can teach us, let us learn willingly—and quickly. It has been said that the Church does not need any individual's contribution. In one sense this is true, for the Church of Christ will not stand or fall on any single person's generosity. Yet it is certainly true that all of us, clergy and people alike, have an inescapable need to give, and to give to the full limit of our ability.

THE NATIONAL COUNCIL OF THE EPISCOPAL CHURCH

The total receipts of the National Council in 1957 were $139,741,450. This was an increase of over $13 million over those reported in 1956, a percentage increase of 10·31%. In February 1958 the National Council adopted the largest budget for its own work in its history, almost $9 million. (This was an increase of $227,000 over actual expenditures and $75,000 more than the annual goal.) This budget may seem small in comparison with the total receipts already mentioned; but one fact needs to be remembered: more than a third of the 7,500 Episcopal churches are missions. These missions are new and small, unable at present to be self-supporting, and they are a diocesan responsibility which modifies the diocesan quotas of the national church budget. The Diocese of Chicago, where I spent much of my time, has 101 parishes and 40 missions; giving to support the missions of the diocese has risen by 85% since 1951.

The National Council is responsible for the full direction of the general programme of the Episcopal Church. The record of the dioceses in striving to meet their assigned share in support of the General Church Programme has been remarkable in recent years. In 1953, for example, 70 out of the 99 dioceses and districts paid or overpaid their quotas, 25 met or bettered their 'expectations', and 4 failed to meet them. In 1956 only 14 failed to meet their quotas in full and 96·8% of the assigned quota was met, compared with 86·5% in 1950. Three-quarters of the budget is for the support of missionary work, at home and abroad, and of the remainder the largest single sum has been for the programme of Christian Education.

In addition to the occasional special campaign, several annual offerings are regularly made throughout the whole Church. Theological Education Sunday has been mentioned already. The success of this offering has been phenomenal. In 1956, only 16 years after its establishment, congregations gave almost half a million dollars to the seminaries. In a very real sense the Theological Education Sunday Offering has made the seminaries truly the care of every church member. If I had not been to a theological college in England, I would not have the slightest idea that any of our seminaries here were in serious financial difficulty. No one has told me!

The 'United Thank Offering' is an accumulation of special gifts from thousands of women in the Episcopal Church during each 3 years. Some idea of the extraordinary increase of this Offering may be gained from the fact that in 1889 the first Offering amounted to a little over $2,000, while in 1952 it was almost $2·5 million and the 1958 triennium ought to close at over $4 million.

One of the latest ventures in financing extraordinary activities in the life and work of the Episcopal Church was the establishment of the Episcopal Church Foundation in 1950. The whole idea was initiated by the Presiding Bishop who saw the Foundation as an opportunity for the Church to attract the kind of gifts it needed to take on big projects above and beyond the regular budget of the Church. The Foundation grants loans free of interest and makes outright gifts to worthy projects. It hopes for an eventual 'capitalization' of $50 million, some of it from small donations. None of the money is deducted for operating expenses. In a single month last year the Foundation released over a million dollars for interest-free construction loans to 58 parishes. Experience indicates that each dollar granted in loans sparks an average $5 worth of new construction. The Unit of Research at Seabury-Western plots the population changes throughout the States so that the Episcopal Church can buy land at the most strategic points for future development. While the Giving is going forward, the Church can go forward. The Presiding Bishop often says, 'If we do it *now*, we'll be strong in 50 years' time.' The Foundation gives immensely valuable assistance to the implementation of the Church's mission from its reservoir of sacrificial and generous donations. This needs stressing because much of American fund-raising is concerned only to be systematic. Whatever the literature may say, plenty of Americans give because they like their church to be businesslike and booming rather than through a true understanding of Christian Giving. The Foundation promotes the sacrificial aspect, which is more important than the systematic.

The Diocesan Departments of Promotion are the essential link between the National Council and the local parishes and missions. Acting closely with the finance department or committee of a diocese or missionary district, the National Council's Field or Promotion Department educates the diocesan family in the principles of stewardship, assists in fixing the diocesan apportionments to the parishes and missions, and promotes the effective use of the Every Member Canvass.

PROFESSIONAL FUND-RAISING

A section on professional fund raising would be helpful before passing to Christian Giving at diocesan and parish level. All of these sections fit together to form the American scene, but there is no logical order. Nevertheless, alongside the Every Member Canvass which is conducted from *within* the Church are professional fund-raising consultants and these can best be discussed at this point. These consultants attract great attention in America and one of them—the Wells Organization—has established offices in England. Others may well do so later. Most of this section is based on American experiences which may reasonably be taken as a guide to what will happen in England if we adopt this type of fund-raising as the best new development.

There are at least twelve major companies conducting capital funds campaigns.[1] They fall into two main categories: those who plan and direct campaigns, using local church folk in the solicitation of giving; and those firms which also bring in trained 'solicitors' to relieve the local church of providing the workers. Each firm makes a set charge for its work, but the basis for the fixed fee varies. Campaign Associates have a minimum charge of $1,800 for a very small church and a maximum charge of $10,000 for a very large church. Cumerford states that the fee charged has no relationship to the goal, but is based on overhead expenses of the campaign, including payment of personnel. This runs from $400 to $600 per man-week. Colonel Wells breaks his explanation down in this way, 'Less than 100 families—two and one-half weeks of service, $1,875-$2,500; 200-275 families—four weeks of service, $3,000-$4,000; 650-800 families—six weeks of service $4,566-$6,000. The variation in fees is explained by seasonal discounts.' Most firms expect a retainer fee, equal to 25% of the total fee, to be paid in advance.

Do any of the fund-raisers give assurance of the success of their campaigns? Most firms do not. They say, 'The responsibility for raising the money must rest with the church—with the firm providing time and experience for guidance and direction.' But Nygaard Associates give guarantees on campaigns of $75,000 and

[1] There are also several hundred smaller companies in existence at any one time.

CHRISTIAN GIVING IN AMERICA

more. Wells Organizations do guarantee success of the effort undertaken. They insure results based on the average results obtained from other churches of the same size and similar giving habits. They also insure 100% collection of the gifts raised at the conclusion of the canvass service.

When is the best time to conduct a professional campaign? Firms divide on this question. Some fund-raisers prefer to conduct the campaign before the building plans (or whatever the project) have been prepared. Wells Organizations have found that 'by conducting the canvass first, the stewardship "concepts of building" can be given proper emphasis. Wells has found that the average family will give more per week, for 100 or 150 weeks, when appealed to on the basis of the need to give.' On the other hand the Ketchum Company challenges *proponents* of early campaigns. The chairman writes: 'Campaigns should follow, not precede, basic decisions by building committees. Church members who can see the preliminary drawings of the new facilities, and who are told of the specific plans of their building committees, give much more understandingly and willingly because they can visualize how their pledges will contribute to the work of the kingdom.'

What is the role of the clergy in these efforts? Here are some condensed replies from firms. 'He must be willing to devote his wholehearted attention to the campaign. This does not interfere with his regular duties.' 'His influence is invaluable in obtaining the campaign leadership . . . he is the ex-officio chairman of all committees, but is not called upon to be the chairman of any committee.' 'To give the same spiritual leadership as he gives to other programmes in his church. He should make a pace-setting pledge which will be an inspiration to members, but he is not singled out for special attention.' Wells Organizations report, 'Let the minister give spiritual leadership; the financial programme rests with the layman. The size of the gift the pastor and family make has great influence on the giving of the others. Many laymen, under guise of sympathy and protection, try to curtail the pastor's giving so they can retain their old habits of token giving.' There is

31

wide variation about publicizing gifts in order to put pressure on others. I quote again from Wells because they have offices in England and are of popular interest. 'Generally gifts are not publicized. However, the announcement of a limited number of pace-setting pledges is an absolutely necessary ingredient in any church canvass which is going to be successful in teaching better habits in giving.'

How much time does it take to put on a campaign? Most of the answers are in man-hours which would include the director and other professional help. The fund-raising agencies are almost unanimous in desiring that no extensive preparations for the campaign be made before their representatives appear on the scene. Campaign Associates estimate that 350 man-hours are necessary for a $100,000 campaign; 500 man-hours for a $200,000 campaign; 700 man-hours for a $500,000 campaign. Thomas White and Associates need 1,200 man-hours for a $100,000 campaign; 1,800 man-hours for a $200,000 campaign; and 3,000 hours for a $500,000 campaign. Wells Organizations say that they require three to four weeks to raise $100,000; five to six weeks to raise $200,000 and eight to ten weeks to raise $500,000. Anyone will agree that no fixed time for a campaign can definitely be set in advance. Too much depends on the local situation. But these figures do represent a reliable appraisal of the amount of man-hours necessary for the professional direction of a fund-raising effort. Each firm gives post-campaign services to its clients.

THE DIOCESE AND CHRISTIAN GIVING

American experiments in Christian Giving are generally not conducted by the odd isolated parish. The liaison between the National Council and the dioceses and its parishes is usually effective enough to make for corporate progress. The role of diocesan headquarters is of the greatest importance because the diocesan authorities advise and direct the parochial clergy. It is obvious that congregations will not understand Christian Giving until the clergy themselves understand and teach their people. Thus a great deal depends on how much—or how little—the diocesan headquarters knows about Christian Giving and fund-raising. In this section two American dioceses will be discussed. They are Chicago and Michigan. They are chosen for different reasons: I lived in Chicago for almost a year, visiting many of its parishes and missions besides the diocesan office; and I have learnt most about how Christian Giving could be promoted in England from the Diocese of Michigan. Both dioceses have progressed far in those aspects of Christian Giving and fund-raising most likely to commend themselves. Both are out in front in their thought and practice and represent situations well ahead of other dioceses, many of whom seemed to be somewhat slow to follow their good example. Every American diocese has a big budget and most have considerable financial problems. But it is important to recognize that these problems are created by vigorous expansion and missionary activity; they are certainly not caused by sloth or lack of intelligent fund-raising. This can be illustrated by reference to many dioceses. For example, the Diocese of West Texas (17,000 baptized members) has adopted a diocesan budget of $290,000 for 1958, of which $55,372 goes to world missionary work and $89,875 to diocesan missionary work. A diocese in full stride is the Diocese of Los Angeles. Its 1958 budget is $756,546, including a missionary budget of $606,181 and a diocesan budget of $150,365: this is an increase of about $50,000 over 1957. An interesting experiment in fund-raising is the Every Member Canvass TV show sponsored by the Diocese of East Carolina. This has proved to be a successful attempt to reach donors by inviting them to hear, in the homes of churchmen, the story of the Church's work in the diocese.

THE DIOCESE OF CHICAGO

The Chicago Diocesan Council handled a budget of almost half a million dollars in 1956, of which $187,000 was the National Council quota. During the same year the parishes and missions of the diocese spent a total of $1,734,500 for new or remodelled churches, rectories, and parish halls. The estimated total giving in the diocese for missionary work in 1958 is $489,590, or $11,000 more than in 1957. As was mentioned earlier, the diocese consists of 101 parishes and 40 missions. The Chicago Department of Promotion has a full-time staff of three and in 1956 cost $13,000 to function. During the year the Department sent out 56,326 diocesan-published pamphlets on Christian Giving. The diocesan magazine for October 1957 included a list of all parishes and missions in the diocese with their 1957 share for missionary giving, the amount pledged by each for 1957 and the payments to September 19th, and 'How does Your Parish Stand?' must have attracted and challenged thousands of church folk.

The most important coin in the Diocese of Chicago is the penny.[1] When offered to God it becomes one of the Bishop's Pence or part of the Children's Lenten Offering. The Children's Offering is a process which goes on throughout the diocese each Lent and comes to a grand climax at a presentation service in the cathedral. 'Mite boxes' for the Offering are filled by hundreds of boys and girls, and these are offered at the altars in local parishes and missions. In 1957 an invitation was issued to every Sunday School in the diocese to be represented by a boy and a girl who respond when the roll of parishes and missions is called. The representatives come forward with a token mite box containing either a statement of the amount of their offering or a cheque for the amount received. In many cases solid study is accompanying the process of sacrificial giving on this juvenile level, as basic principles of stewardship are inculcated and the vision of missionary strategy is caught.

Training children to give is of the greatest importance. Children cannot be expected to give to God until they understand why and how. One of the major reasons why many church folk in England 'tip' God with the smallest coin would seem to be that false concepts of Christian Giving are bred and encouraged in Sunday

[1] The small copper one-cent coin, about the size of our farthing, and in purchasing power equivalent to a half-penny.

school. Children grow up believing that God should be given the smallest coin or nothing at all because this is tolerated week after week in Sunday school. There are many examples of this 'toleration' but among the most popular are: no explanation of Christian Giving; no appeal to the children's imagination; no idea that the offertory is an act of worship. Recently I attended a meeting in an active middle-class parish in London. The Sunday school accounts were read and greeted with prolonged applause. True and commendable were the facts that they were up on the previous year and that 25s. weekly was sent to the CMS; but while we confine ourselves to statistics of this sort we shall go on mistakenly applauding our own generosity. Those who were congratulating the Sunday school for its contributions were oblivious of the fact that these represented a penny farthing per week for every child and teacher.

Many examples could be cited of how we applaud our own meanness under the impression it is generosity. Here is one. I was shown the other day the accounts of an active residential parish. The receipts were over £2,500, of which over £700 (almost 30% of the total receipts) was given to causes outside the parish. Thus the parish is giving out about £14 weekly, and the Parochial Church Council passed the accounts as 'very creditable'. So they are, until the all-important question is asked: how much is the parish *receiving* from outside sources? (In order to facilitate frank assessment of the giving of any congregation, *all income other than from living members and friends of the congregation* should be considered as coming from outside sources.) This was not shown on the budget; but the parish was in fact receiving more than the £700 it was giving, and apparently nobody realized it! This is a parish whose members presume themselves to be not only self-supporting, but contributing £14 weekly to the Church at large; they seem to be oblivious of the fact that it is they themselves who are dependent on the Church at large.

This is not so in America. Most American clergy realize that the Church cannot afford to be mean; so they train their people to give. Special attention is paid to the training of Sunday school children *and teachers*. Young minds are caught and taught by excellent films, film-strips and comic-strips, as well as by the spoken word. In Chicago there is an annual Bishop's Pence Poster contest. In 1957 over a thousand posters were made by the children of the diocese. There were three age groups and forty-four prizes. More than two-thirds of the parishes participated and submitted an average of fifteen entries each.

So far the Bishop's Pence have been mentioned but not discussed. This programme had its beginnings in the great economic depression of the 'thirties. At that time the Bishop of Chicago, 'with discouraged and disheartened people, with shrinking financial resources and beset by calls from all sides for assistance, proposed the idea of regular corporate grace at mealtimes with the offering of a small gift from each member of the family at meal-times'. There were many in Chicago—as there would be in England—who doubted the long-term usefulness of the Bishop's Pence. Many felt it was a fad which would disappear after a few years.

Twenty-five years have proved these prophets to be entirely wrong, for each succeeding year has seen the programme grow in effectiveness. 1957 was the thirteenth consecutive record-setting year, during which $65,000 was received. Total returns are almost a million dollars. Half of the net proceeds go to the Bishop and the other half to participating churches. The Bishop's share has helped buy land for new missions, has helped with building programmes, has provided a fund for a new altar for the cathedral and has assisted many in trouble. Congregations have used their share for innumerable things—choir vestments, music, altars, vestments, organs, prayer books. The present Bishop of Chicago has described the influence of the programme in the following ways: (1) The underlying purpose to educate our people to say grace at mealtime has made a real spiritual contribution to the life of the diocese. The good habit of returning thanks has been firmly established in many homes. (2) The Pence Programme has done much to develop a spirit of corporateness in the diocese. Especially among the laity, the regular meetings of Pencemen and the strong friendships that have been made by such contacts have established a feeling of belonging to a Church that is a greater unit than the congregation. (3) The Pence Programme has convinced the person of small resources that small gifts 'count' in the corporate life of the Church. More than 75,000,000 thank offerings have helped to extend the work of our Lord in many places. This is a way in which every family can share in the work of the Church, help them acquire land or church buildings.

This programme has succeeded in a wonderful way because it was well-launched. In the modern world the Church will not normally achieve big things for God by thinking and planning in small and petty ways. Not all of the Church's work is 'big' but its resources are and it needs to use them effectively. The Bishop's Pence was officially launched in October 1933 by sending approximately 20,000 Pence cans, accompanied by a descriptive leaflet, through the post to the families of the diocese. It had been preceded by a fanfare of publicity with stories in the Church and secular press, special Pence sermons by the clergy, and so on. Bishop Stewart set the ideal when he said, 'The Bishop's Pence has gone into the home and says don't eat as if *you* had made the food: eat and be thankful that God gave it to you.' In the first year returns exceeded $28,000 and 'enabled us to save our missionary and social service work from wreckage.' The idea spread like wild-fire and enquiries poured into the Pence Office from all over the world. In 1934 the General Convention of the Episcopal Church adopted the following resolution: 'Be it resolved that the House of Deputies, the House of Bishops concurring, endorses the plan of Bishop's Pence as a means of bringing into our family life prayer and thanksgiving for God's mercies and the regular and persistent practice of giving, three times each day, a token of one penny; and recommends to all dioceses, parishes, missions and institutions the adoption of this plan.'

Since those days almost a million dollars has been given and the diocese and its people have grown materially and spiritually. All of this large amount of money is income which otherwise would not have found its way to the Church. It was not obtained at the expense of regular giving. Perhaps above all, the Bishop's Pence have given the diocese a sense of corporateness, a feeling of working together for the glory of God, from the most far-flung mission on the perimeter to the venerable parish in the inner city.

THE DIOCESE OF MICHIGAN

Chicago and Michigan have several things in common. Both dioceses believe in long-range planning. The vision of Bishop Stewart and the Pence Programme has been mentioned; while up in Michigan today Bishop Emrich frequently speaks and writes about 'the diocese in 1970'. This long-term planning is of great importance, especially in the sphere of Christian Giving, and the time-factor in the strategy of both dioceses deserves serious consideration: the more so in England, where many Christians appear to have had little or no training in Christian Giving.

A second similarity between Michigan and Chicago is the willingness to learn in order to make sound progress. I wrote elsewhere, 'The outstanding characteristic of the American Church is its refusal to accept defects as irremediable. I saw this most clearly when discussing English church problems. Often Americans said, "What's all the delay over there? Why don't you get the show on the road? What are you all waiting for?" ' It seems that Chicago and Michigan are out in front because clergy and people are so willing to learn and go out of their way to seek for advice and improvements. Both dioceses realize that *people do not give as they are able but as they understand*. The crux of Christian Giving is that it is a process of teaching and learning, and these dioceses are ahead because they have proved this. To this approach is linked the fact that diocesan fund-raising is run by diocesan headquarters. The work of the Church is directed by the diocesan authorities rather than by an outside professional firm.

The main similarity between Chicago and Michigan is the emphasis on the fact that Christian Giving is a spiritual practice.

38

This statement underlines a gradual but definite change in the discussion from '*How* does the Church raise its money?' to '*Why* do Christians give so much?' This change defies strict description because of the variety of the American scene. For more than half my year I 'lapped up' American techniques of fund-raising. They are effective and systematic; they enlist lay support and get splendid results; there are professional fund-raisers who will come into the parish and do the job properly. This commended itself in a big way, mainly, I suppose, because I have the type of mind which adores 'know-how' and the strictly practical approach. At the same time this was my fourth year of academic theology and I was much concerned with the need for 'theology' in Christian strategy. This dual approach led to an admiration of American techniques and an awareness that they would probably not work nor commend themselves in England.

This digression from Chicago and Michigan is deliberate. It may be easy to feel that fund-raising firms deserve more sympathy and understanding or that any criticism of them is vague and unfounded.[1] It is at this point that the practices in Chicago and Michigan assume their importance. These dioceses approach Christian Giving as primarily a spiritual practice rather than as an efficient system. The doubts about professional fund-raising, even of schemes commended by the Episcopal National Council and the National Council of Churches, appear in their sharpest form when held in contrast to the practice in the Diocese of Michigan.[2] It was knowledge of this programme which provided the 'break-through' in my own thinking. I believe that the Diocese of Michigan has found the right way to promote Christian Giving and that all other techniques are less worthy by comparison.

Bishop Emrich and his Diocese would probably indignantly repudiate the implication that they have either discovered Christian Giving or Modern Tithing for the first time, or have developed

[1] My own view of the place of professional fund-raising firms will be found in the Appendix, pp. 83-86.

[2] Though see p. 83.

it further or faster than others. It was their experience and their methods, however, which opened my own eyes. Furthermore, that Diocese seems to be a strange and almost incompatible mixture of wealthy urban communities, small towns and rural areas, and giant urban-industrial centres. Thus the effectiveness of experiments in Michigan gives the lie to those in other parts of the country who would say 'Oh, it won't work here because. . . .'

In this section the thought and practice inspired by the Diocesan Office in Detroit is reported so closely that it is not possible to list individual references. But I have acknowledged my indebtedness and gratitude to the Bishop and to the Department of Promotion in the Introduction. They have seen Christian Giving in action throughout a whole diocese and their programme is no longer a conjecture but something *which has happened already*. And perhaps no influence in church life is more powerful than the influence of other people's actual experiences. No evidence is more conclusive. This *has happened* in dioceses and parishes like ours.

The Rt Rev. R. S. M. Emrich became the seventh Bishop of Michigan in 1948 at the age of thirty-eight. He had been previously Suffragan and then Coadjutor Bishop of the diocese. The fact that he has been Bishop in Michigan since 1946 is significant because Christian Giving, whether on parish or diocesan level, is a long-term programme. From Bishop Emrich came the inspiring and basic religious idea—to resurrect and put into effect in every parish of the diocese the Biblical idea of tithing. Here, at long last was a historically sound basis which every Episcopalian could adopt to determine how much he should give to God in return for what God has given him. Actually to 'tithe' is to give one-tenth of one's income to the Church. But the Bishop, with wise appreciation of present income taxes and the need to support 'outside' charities which once came under the province of the Church, has proposed the following idea: Let every Episcopalian adopt in gratitude to God the idea of devoting one-tenth of his net income (after income taxes) to selfless purposes—5% for his church and 5% for general charities.

Before discussing how this idea has been developed into a diocesan programme, it would be helpful to include a short selection of remarks made by Bishop Emrich during a recent lecture to New York clergy on 'Stewardship' (and quoted by kind permission): 'When I first entered the ministry, I dreaded speaking to people about money. I had within me that reluctance which you have certainly seen in yourself, and very evidently in some at least of your vestry (parochial church council). I had the mistaken idea that the spiritual and material worlds were somehow divided, that it was my task to deal with things spiritual, the vestry's task to deal with material, and that somehow I lowered myself and was placed in an embarrassing position when I was forced to ask people for their money. And, since I have lived through this embarrassment and come out on the other side, I have no doubt that the failure of the Church financially in some parishes is due to this false reticence on the part of some clergy in speaking about money. But I soon came to see that this attitude of mine was a serious mistake—was indeed, when considered at its deepest level, a great religious error, a heresy. . . .

'The importance of money can be seen in that most crimes involve it. Therefore, the Son of God, bringing truth to men, had to speak about it. And gladly, therefore, we speak about it. What an irrelevant and silly religion, incapable of redeeming this world, it would be if it ignored this part of life that is so important to men. Men handle it day in and day out, have it in their pockets, waste it, kill for it, sell their souls for it—and some clergy so misunderstand God's purposes that they are embarrassed to speak of it!'

And again, in two further extracts of great insight and significance, Bishop Emrich said: 'We do not primarily want money. We want souls that are dedicated to God, souls that are converted and hence God's stewards, souls that read their Scripture and say their prayers. If we have money without that, we are dead. If we have devotion we'll have the money. We will be timid in speaking to people about their money only if we are timid in asking them in full seriousness to give their souls to God. It's the old, old matter of seeking first the Kingdom of God and as a result having other things added unto us. . . .

'I cannot tell any man how much to give to church and charity in dollars and cents, for I do not know that much about any man; but I do not have the slightest hesitation in asking a man to give as God has given to him, which is the principle of proportionate giving or tithing. Nor do I have the slightest hesitation in asking men to be thankful and responsible to God, and to reveal this, not only with their lips but in their lives. And I do not have the slightest hesitation in saying that it seems to me absurd that an institution the size of the Episcopal Church has given its people no practical advice on *how* to give. This practice of proportionate giving or tithing must begin with the bishops and clergy, for we would not want to preach what we are not trying to practise. The best way to teach any practice is a quiet personal witness about what it means to us.'

These words of wisdom will commend themselves to all who are concerned with Christian Giving in England. Bishop Emrich has focussed on motives and principles as the only Christian basis for diocesan progress, and these are of universal application. They apply to Christians everywhere, as much in any English diocese as in Michigan. In past years many folk in Michigan had been talking about tithing in terms of what it would do for anyone who seriously gave it a try. The tone, up to this point, was 'If you will try tithing, we *believe* this is what will happen to you'. That was some time ago. Now those same folk can say: 'This is *what has happened* to many people who have tried it.' No one need conjecture any more. And just for this record, the total annual receipts of the Diocese of Michigan are among the highest per living donor in the United States.

Christian Giving on a diocesan scale was launched by Bishop Emrich in an address in September 1950. He took off from a quotation which formed the serious background against which diocesan strategy should be measured—'If we have learned anything, it is that the Marxist movement is dynamic. That seems to be the only word: *dynamic*. It has shown it has the power of religion to move millions and to call forth human loyalties, heroisms, and sacrifices that might otherwise have gone untapped. It is able to inspire, to invigorate, to sweep across a people—as it has in Asia—and feed on the highest aspirations of existence by half-way measures. We can, and should, protect ourselves from it by force of arms, but we cannot drive it out of existence that way. *It has the force and appeal of religion and only another equally dynamic religion can replace it.*' Against that background, the Bishop maintained, no one would object to completely serious thinking, to self-criticism and to a new policy over the whole diocese. 'We are gathered here today concerned with Church finance, without which the Church cannot go forward. Let us be critical of ourselves, and then state the new programme.'

Bishop Emrich's analysis is set out in full. 'The chief method by which your parish or mission raises its budget is the Every Member Canvass. The good and necessary thing about the Canvass is that every year you strive to reach everyone in your Church community for a responsible pledge. All of us would agree that is essential. But who will deny that there is something wrong somewhere with what we do? All of us have felt this, even though we have never analysed it carefully. Let me list some of the weaknesses, because when we see what is wrong it helps us to see what is right.

'(1) We make our Canvass year after year without conveying real teaching or a sense of responsibility to thousands and thousands of our people. One would think that this much organization, this much printed material, and this much real effort would leave lasting religious teaching. But somehow it does not.

'(2) Another weakness is that for two or three weeks in the autumn we go into a kind of flurry and frenzy, and then do practically nothing for the remaining fifty weeks. We cannot always be canvassing, but some more indirect form of education should be carried on all year long. Two or three weeks in the autumn

43

is not sufficient, and every thinking person will agree with this.

'(3) Still another weakness is that we go to our people chiefly with a budget. We draw up an inadequate budget, and then ask the people to meet this inadequate budget which has no necessary relationship to their ability to give. But those of us who know the Diocese know that many of our Churches need more clergy; that 50% of our clergy are underpaid; that new areas in Michigan and the world are crying for new men; and that there are numerous needs not provided for in the budget. Yes, there is something wrong in drawing up an inadequate budget, and then asking people to meet this inadequate budget which is unrelated to their ability to give.

'(4) Our weakness is revealed further when you analyse the income figures in your parish or mission. You will find that about 25% of your people give 80% of the budget! In brief, the trouble with the present system is not that we try to reach everyone with a canvass—that is good! The trouble is that in full seriousness throughout the year we do not teach our people *how* to give. We have had no standard. We have no standard that we speak of year in and year out, until in big talk and in small talk everyone knows of it. In our present system we have no standard that comes from the heart of the faith and goes to the heart of every member of the Church.

'Now, given these weaknesses, one of the tasks of a bishop is to form a policy to make universal in the Diocese practices which are sound religiously and will help to overcome these problems. I would like, therefore, to outline for you our new Diocesan policy. This policy is not really new: it has been tried and tested in Michigan by one of our large parishes which has the best record proportionately of any Church in the Diocese. Many minds in many parishes, facing the same problem, have arrived independently at the necessity for a standard, the necessity for proportionate giving. Above all, it has the backing of Scripture and of practice in the Church. It was the practice, you know, in the Old Testament to give 10% of one's income to God. This practice was

44

undoubtedly used by our Lord and in his life he certainly went far beyond it. He said that "not one jot nor one tittle" was to be taken from the law, and told his followers that their "righteousness (was to) exceed that of the Scribes and the Pharisees". One of the purposes of rules and laws and standards is to show people what responsibility means. However, the ancient Tithe is not realistic for us today, because so many of the charities once conducted by the Temple or the Church are now carried on by the community. What is realistic today is 5% of one's income for the community Fund, Red Cross, and special drives; and 5% for the Church. The realistic plan today is, in brief, to continue our Every Member Canvasses—and then, in season and out, all year long, in small groups and large, to teach this standard as a guide for all people. It comes from the heart of the faith and goes in complete seriousness to the heart of the believer.'

The pattern for Christian Giving which has emerged in the Diocese of Michigan is based on nine reasons for Modern Tithing:

1. It guides us by providing us with a method of intelligent giving.
2. It helps us by freeing our church leaders from a preoccupation with money for the more important task of ministering to people.
3. It places us all, rich or poor, on an equal footing before God.
4. It helps us by enabling our Church to speak not about money in a begging attitude, but about responsibility in a dignified manner.
5. It shows us in a concrete manner the everyday meaning of real gratitude to God for the many things he has given to us.
6. By making us responsible with a fixed percent of our income, it teaches us responsibility in the handling of all our possessions.
7. Like all truly Christian living, it brings to us the joy of an honest and important participation in God's work in this world.

8. It places us in a mighty tradition because it has Scriptural authority.

9. It helps us to see that all of living, even the making of a personal budget and the spending of money, can be done to God's glory.

Don't miss the point! Tithing is *not* a money-raising scheme nor a tax. It is the right and serious way to give. It is not primarily a means for raising money, nor is it a substitute for other methods of getting money to meet church obligations. Rather, Tithing is a returning to God of a small but definite part of the many gifts received from his hands—a token payment of gratitude. Tithing teaches; 'tipping' does not. And the man who knows that God is the central fact of life, who feels the daily nearness of God, who sees the constant evidence of God's love and who offers himself in gratitude to God, this man is a transformed man. Therefore, don't miss the point! The purpose of Tithing is to secure not the tithe but the tither; not the gift but the giver; not the possession but the possessor; not your money but you—for God.

How does all this work out in the parish? The Michigan Department of Promotion has experienced that the sequence below is the proper one and that there will be a loss of effectiveness if an attempt is made to pass over the preliminary steps.

First Year. The Bishop introduced the subject of Tithing to the Every Member Canvass parish chairmen at their autumn meeting. The theme of the Canvass this year was 'A Better Way'. The better way was: giving in relation to one's income and not in relation to a budget. A layman's endorsement of the 'better way' was printed in a pamphlet entitled, *What shall I Give?* and given the largest possible circulation in the diocese. A sound film was made following the outline of *What shall I Give?* and circulated throughout the diocese.

The object was to change the orientation of our people. They had always thought, and been taught to think about their duty of supporting the budget of parish, diocese and National Church.

The Church had always couched its promotion in the seller's terms: 'If you do what we suggest, the Church will benefit.' Now we put it in buyer's terms. Our purpose this year was to get them to think only about 'How the individual grows in grace through grateful and responsible use of money.'

Second Year. The meeting of the Canvass Chairmen from the parishes, formerly held in the autumn, was moved up to June. This was done to allow the parishes a longer interim period for planning and perfecting this Canvass organization. An Educational Chairman was added as an assistant to the General Chairman in each parish. The reason for this was that in the past the Chairman's job had been only to see to the mechanics of organization and execution. In Tithing, a new element, that of 'idea content' is introduced, and the canvassers' training becomes a two-fold task. The General Chairman was given a printed guide to help him to: (1) Induce the parochial church council to support the principle of giving in relation to income. (2) Orientate the parish. For this purpose he was also provided with certain tools beside the guide: the film, group discussion guides, suggestions for parish suppers. (3) Train the canvassers. The theme of this second year was 'Don't Miss the Point', which was also the title of a printed piece which was given general circulation. The 'point' that was not to be missed was: 'Tithing is not for the good of the Church's budget, but for the good of *your* soul.'

Third Year. The new element this year was the result of a survey made among people in varying parishes where Tithing had gone on for a year or more. From the experiences of these people a testimonial pamphlet, *A Christian Budget For Family Security*, was compiled and circulated throughout the diocese. The theme this year was 'Now We Know'. The Department of Promotion was no longer promoting a theory, but now had the word of people who in actual practice found that Tithing had the power to change their lives. A printed calendar, with seven steps recommended for organizing the Canvass, was provided for the General Chairman. The purpose of this calendar was to put before the Chairman, in concise form, the proper time sequence for him to follow. Also the Department developed a film-strip, in cartoon style, entitled 'The Case of the Not-So-Busy Canvasser', and parishes used it in training canvassers in how to make a Tithing call.

Fourth Year. By now it was clear that some places were not able to train Canvass workers adequately, so the Department stressed *pre-drilling* parishioners *before* the Canvass. Two sample Tithing letters were provided for parishes to use as mailings and the Bishop wrote a pastoral letter which was used all over the diocese. The theme this year was that 'Tithing is a Logical Derivative of Basic Christian Doctrine'. It was felt that the diocese had made enough progress to base the main printed piece, 'How to Use Your Money', on the theology of Tithing.

Fifth Year. At this stage a solid majority of parishes basing their Canvass on Tithing had been established. The Department sent them printed pieces and let them go to work. Then it concentrated on the non-Tithing minority, with trained laymen, using a new turn-over chart presentation. They met with parochial church councils in June and with Canvass workers in the autumn. The theme was, 'The Policy Makers of the Parish Must Back Tithing, and Parish Tithers Must Witness to It.' The printed pieces dealt with 'The Real Meaning of Thanksgiving and Questions and Answers about Tithing.'

Sixth Year. The Department of Promotion felt that more work was needed on the mechanics of getting Tithing adopted, so the literature concentrated on this. To reach young people aged 8-14, a comic book was created; to get adults committed a 'new Tither's card' was included in their brochure; to improve the parish's education, a guide on the whys and wherefores of a year-round Tithing Commission was produced. The theme was, 'To Be Effective, Tithing Must Be Taught at Every Stage of Parish Life.'

Seventh Year. With a background of six years in the teaching of Tithing, it was felt that by now many church members needed

Campus Crusade for Christ Library

only the inspiration to make a decision. The Canvass Chairmen, *and clergy*, were gathered in June for this. The new booklet, *From Whom No Secrets Are Hid*, was designed to supply this inspiration. Its companion at Sunday School level is another cartoon booklet, *Mummy—Why Does God Need Money?*, and the theme was: 'Now is the Time for Decision.'

This programme deserves the fullest consideration in England. There can be no doubt that this is the right and serious way to train our people to give. It is being tried on a small scale in various English parishes and to encourage others, some points of the Michigan scheme are enlarged. These further observations are based on the combined experiences of over a hundred missions and parishes of all signs, shapes and varieties, over a period of more than five years.

This experience points to an important conclusion: To teach Tithing effectively you must have a year-round Tithing Commission at parochial and diocesan levels. But why year-round? To accomplish any worthwhile project requires a constant continuous teaching effort. And making clear in the minds of all parishioners that they are only stewards of God's gifts, helps to establish Tithing as a normal part of parish life. Teaching all the year round will reach new members of the parish soon after their joining, instead of waiting for what might be many months. Parish life goes on all year-round, so should parish information; and to change the deep-seated habit of 'tipping' God requires more than a fortnight's flurry.

How is this established in a parish? It is of the utmost importance that the principle of Tithing has the official endorsement of the clergy and parochial church council. The council can adopt some resolution supporting Tithing as the 'right standard for Christian Giving'. (This does not commit any individual.) Then the PCC sets up a Tithing Commission to teach this principle, with representatives (serving a limited term in rotation) from each functioning church organization. It is important that regular Tithing Commission meetings should be held. There should be a thorough discussion of ideas, approaches and methods, and reports should be made by each member on work done. A concrete parish education plan should be drawn up on paper, and all channels of communication utilized to reach people so that there is a steady flow of information on Christian Giving. Folk will accept Tithing as the basis of giving only if they understand it thoroughly.

Especially important is the inclusion of Tithing education as a *regular part* of confirmation instruction and the Sunday school curriculum. It needs to be part of the parish programme for Lent. There should be periodic sermons—not just one a year—on Christian gratitude, stewardship and Tithing. Some American parishes have occasional lay-sermons on these subjects and find personal testimonies the most powerful convincer. And frequent use should be made of the parish magazine and other literature to carry short provocative paragraphs on Modern Tithing. Reference was made earlier to the Chicago diocesan magazine which listed the progress of every parish and mission. Finally, each new person in the parish should be called on by a Tithing Commission member so that newcomers learn the principle of Tithing as soon as possible.

What can we expect? Tithing taught even on a part-time basis has worked, but not nearly as well as where it is a year-round programme. It takes several consecutive years of concerted effort to achieve a wide understanding and adoption of Tithing—and even then there will be some who never will. Results will not come overnight. Yet there will develop a greatly increased commitment to the Lord, not only in the giving of money, but also of time and talents. This means that the *primary result* of Tithing is in the changing of human lives, not in the resulting increase in parish income. Tithing unites and helps build strong parishes by establishing a common ground for giving together, and as more people adopt Tithing as a basis of giving, it will affect the giving of non-Tithers. Church members, whose period of service on the Tithing Commission has ended, become missionaries for the idea within the congregation. Thus the vicar and parochial church council are freed from endless haggling about money for the more important task of really ministering to people.

AMONG PARISHES AND MISSIONS

Tithing in the Diocese of Michigan has been developed along the lines indicated in the previous section. But very little has been written about the parishes and missions scattered throughout the States which have no diocesan supervision similar to that in Michigan. These parishes and missions also succeed in Christian Giving, although often with assistance of fund-raising firms, and do indicate that some progress can be made irrespective of diocesan planning. The principles of Christian Giving adopted throughout Michigan can be practised by any parish, but in other parts of the States are parishes and missions which are stirring their congregations to give and these, too, have ideas and encouragement to pass on. It is wonderful inspiration to visit churches which can truly claim that parish building now equals parish spirit and to meet people who do not have to think in terms of 'when we can have a new hall' or 'when the Church school can be rebuilt'. Soon after my arrival in Evanston, Professor R. H. Fuller and I were shown over the parish plant of St Matthew. The new parish house and religious education building has 12 classrooms, a dining room for 250 and an assembly hall for 250. We were amazed at the effective striking power of a parish which thought and acted on this scale—and our amazement amazed them!

St Matthew is a large and active parish, but progress on lower levels is equally inspiring. Just as I was leaving Chicago five *small missions* in the diocese established stewardship records which should challenge every parish, large as well as small. These five congregations had a total membership of 511 and they increased their giving from $28,101 to $71,208. This represents an increase of 153% over amounts previously pledged. Perhaps most significant of all, these missions are now able to become self-supporting, thus releasing more funds to expand the missionary programme of the Episcopal Church.

Thus parishes and small missions are growing in grace through corporate giving. Here is an extract from a Family Eucharist service sheet (not in the Diocese of Michigan): 'It is not just a pious formality to have the men of our parishes bring the money offerings of our people to the parish altar for presentation and blessing. This is the manner and the place in which we express our parish trusteeship. We offer our gifts to Almighty God, from whom they have come to us, and we receive them back both with his blessing and with his charge to us that we distribute them consistent with the mode of our offering. Whether the cash pays the fuel bills or the priest's salary, or is used for grass seed or Sunday School equipment, we should not lose sight of these as all being ways of giving to the glory of God and for the spread of his kingdom. If we benefit directly, the benefit has Christian significance only as we accept it as an aid of our own stewardship.'

American congregations are beginning to realize that parish giving approaches Christian standards when all the people subscribe to and support the principle of giving without any expectation of enjoying the benefit of their gifts. This means to give outside at least as much as would be liked for parish use; to give without the assurance of seeing the results; to offer gifts to God trusting that he will achieve good things 'which exceed all that we can desire'. Congregations who are being taught along these lines are growing in grace and in their share in spreading God's kingdom. And the reverse is manifestly true; that congregations are failing and falling by the wayside whenever clergy and people are content to 'tip' God.

In America the responsibility of the parish for the work of the Church outside the local parish has been based for many years now (since the thirties) on the 'Partnership Principle'—roughly a 50-50 division between local needs and spending, and extra-parochial (diocesan, national, missionary).[1] The parish I attended

[1] In the Episcopal Church in the USA, as in the Church of Scotland, missionary work is run by the Church, and there is not our variety of independent missionary societies.

in Evanston, for example, has adhered to this even during the darkest days of the depression. This raises the question: What goes at the top of the parish budget? Its own needs *or* the spread of Christ's Kingdom? It seems that the 'Partnership Principle' has been and is followed by the 'best' dioceses. No matter how urgent and pressing the local demands, they share 50-50 with the National Council. I am told that on the diocesan level the principle has not been followed as rigidly (proportionately) as it should have been. *And*, a diocese which 'short-changes' the National Council and other national responsibilities cannot exert the moral influence it might on its own parishes and missions.

On the whole, American lay-folk are catching on to real Christian Giving. But it is neither easy nor overnight in application. For example one problem which confronts the young, fast-growing suburban parish is its young, fast-growing missionary quota. The suburban PCC is stunned, year after year, to discover that the missionary demands of the diocese and national Church seem insatiable. A 15% increase in 1955 became a 20% increase in 1956, and a 22% increase in 1957. Not only must the parish meet its own enlarged budget year after year; it must increase its giving to the Church's needs outside the parish at the same time. Only thus can the Church take a vigorous part in meeting the needs and opportunities of modern life. And thus, in actual fact, missions that began with tiny handfuls become thriving parishes in a few years, and in a few years more are nearing the 1,000 communicant class with curates and full-time directors of Christian education. This is happening throughout the States and churches, educational buildings and rectories are springing up like mushrooms. Thus the whole Church is grappling with the challenge of modern life and *expanding* in so doing. But this would be impossible on 'tips'. It is possible only by congregations giving to the glory of God, 'from whom no secrets are hid'.

THE ENGLISH SCENE

THE English scene is difficult to assess. Much is being done to promote Christian Giving. For the first time there is widespread interest in the possibilities of professional fund-raising by outside firms. At almost every level of church life incomes are rising steadily and consistently and this is accompanied by spiritual growth. There is an increasing awareness that if we can solve financial difficulties, we shall derive fresh encouragement and impetus in solving other problems. This awareness is evident in many aspects of diocesan and parochial strategy, and alongside all the appeals in the religious press are frequent details of experiments in fund-raising. In these directions, and many others throughout the country, people are rediscovering the meaning of Stewardship. This is a real sign that we are growing in grace and indicates that our opportunities for advance are as valuable a potential for God as those in the United States or elsewhere. Certainly this present discussion is not a denial that Christian Giving is not going on day by day in parish after parish: rather it is intended as part of the search for greater endeavour and clarity of thought, based on the conviction that the resources for these are to hand up and down the country.

At the same time one is bound to return from a year in the States full of American 'methodology'. As soon as one tries to grapple with the application of these insights, one quickly realizes how alert the Church is. Nevertheless, it must be obvious to all of us that Christian Giving at least is one sphere in which we have a great deal to learn before our churches can plan and expand as they ought. Anyone who studies the principal developments in Christian Giving in England during the past fifty years will be amazed at the number of official committees and excellent reports which seem to have had little or any practical effect in the parishes. In 1957 the total receipts from living donors in the Episcopal Church were 10·31% higher than in the previous year. But in England there must be very few spheres in which the spread of the Gospel is not restricted by the lack of Christian Giving: indeed, it is important to compare frequently the expansion and restriction of the Church in reaching every area of life. Many instances of our strange values in this country could be given. Sufficient to think about, perhaps, is the fact that CMS finds it difficult to raise £600,000 annually among a people who spend more than £40 million a year on food for their pets; and that in Britain in 1957 we saved between 10 and 11% of personal income after tax. The money is there all right! (Personal income rose 8% in 1956 and 5½% in 1957.)

The present discussion seeks to balance the 'know-how' and the 'know-why'. The basis of Christian Giving is right here: that church people should know how and why to give. Too much of our thinking is based on the assumption that our Lord has promised us something for nothing. 'What you clergy must do,' a young man told me recently, 'is to find a painless way of extracting money from people. We've got the cash and you've got to get it—only it must be painless.' Such a view is alarmingly common. And, as I have mentioned elsewhere, I have heard two or three sermons every week for years, but I have never heard an English clergyman preach on Christian Giving. I have been amazed at the number who admit that it has never occurred to them to preach on this aspect of the Christian life. Nevertheless, the need for sermons on Giving is becoming recognized at all levels and many congregations are now hearing them for the first time. This is a great step towards solving this problem from the inside. As a result there are congregations up and down the country who are contributing goodly sums each week in spite of the general economic situation. I used to think that the clergy should teach and practise Christian Giving until it hurts. One day someone pointed out that this would *not* be Christian Giving at all.

Christian Giving does not begin until it begins to hurt. 'Give until it hurts' is sub-Christian; 'Give when it hurts' should be our standard. Less than this is not *giving* in any meaningful way for the giver.

In recent years we have been able to enjoy an increasing number of books passing on ideas for contemporary evangelism and analysing the present religious climate. Such books are a great help and I have been fortunate to read many of them. But I disagree with one implication, which in most cases is but a passing observation, but which in this discussion is of great concern. This implication is that our comparative failures in Christian Giving are due largely to lay-folk.

Canon Eaton, for example, writes: 'Giving of money is an important part of the practice of our Churchmanship, and I regret to have to record that the present members of the Church of England are notoriously bad givers, and it has all arisen because modern Churchmen have never seriously thought out their duty and responsibility for this part of the Kingdom of Heaven.'[1] Has it all arisen in this way? Or has it arisen because the clergy are not training their people how and why to give? This idea that the laity are the real cause of church financial problems is a dangerous half-truth. There seems to be no evidence either side of the Atlantic that congregations will really give until and unless they are taught to give. It is difficult to frown on anyone for not being trained to give. Put briefly, 'tipping' God springs from toleration; Tithing springs from teaching. Here again one of the great truths about Christian Giving is underlined; that people give, not as they are able, but as they understand.

No attempt is being made in this section to list or discuss parishes or dioceses which are well on the way to solving financial problems. Great progress is being made in a few parts of the country, but such activity is not sufficiently widespread to be characteristic of the English religious scene. It is very doubtful if

[1] A. W. Eaton: *The Faith, History and Practice of the Church of England* (Hodder and Stoughton), p. 135.

overseas visitors would include Christian Giving as one of the lessons to be learned from the Church in England. But what is characteristic is the great concern about Christian Giving evident in all parts of the country. This statement is made largely because of the many folk who have approached me for further information. Many queries have been raised, though no disagreements, and it would seem proper to deal with these in this section. For these are the characteristic questions actually being asked about Christian Giving by clergy and lay-folk up and down the country. They are genuine; there are no fictional questions nor conjectural answers. These queries concern the principles of Giving, and it is important to clarify our motives. Much of our parochial fund-raising is based on suspect principles, which are detached from a theological and Biblical basis and from the spiritual growth of the congregation. The Diocese of Michigan has proved conclusively that the only way ahead is to get the principles of Christian Giving straight.

There is real danger here. Too much of our thinking about money on this side of the Atlantic is sub-Christian. Our principles are often wrong. We are often far more concerned with fund-raising than with Christian Giving. How often does the Church appeal for money? How rarely does the Church teach about it? This leads to the further consideration: *How much of our church income is from Christian Giving?* There can be no set answer, but any estimate must allow for the following points: (1) That less than half the present income of the Church comes from *living* donors. Seven-eighths of our clergy salaries are paid by previous generations of Christians. If we appreciated the wealth we inherit, we might be less inclined to complain about the upkeep of historic churches. (2) Many contributors to Sunday collections are 'tipping' God. This is not Christian Giving. (3) Large proportions of parish incomes are raised by 'begging' and other unworthy means of raising money. This is not Christian Giving. I can only conclude that folk who resent the terms 'tipping' God and 'begging for' God have never thought out the principles of Christian

Giving. How apt is a remark made to me in the States, 'Most of your church-goers over there are riding free!'

Here, then, are the questions being asked by clergy and lay-folk in England to-day. And here are some of the answers from families like ours, parishes like ours, who have *proved* that through a Christian budget they have grown in faith and in grace and in the satisfaction of extending God's Kingdom. This is not a theory any more! Did not St Paul say, 'Now as you excel in everything— in faith, in utterance, in knowledge, in all earnestness, and in your love for us—see that you excel in this gracious work also? (II Cor. 8.6).

WHAT IS TITHING?

Tithing is an open-hearted act of living gratitude. It is the result of a Christian decision to say, 'Thank You, Lord', each day in a faithful way for the countless blessings which come from him, including the precious gift of life itself. The ancient Biblical Tithe was a straight 10% of all that a person received. The Modern Tithe asks each Christian person or family to give (after Income Tax is deducted): 5% for the Lord through the Church as an act of self-giving—in obedience to the first and great commandment; and 5% to charity for the needs of others in Christian obedience to the second and great commandment. As Bishop Emrich says, 'Certainly our Church is reasonable in its standard of 5% of net income to God—to God who gave us life—the intelligence and ability to earn—the health to enjoy a profitable life—and the opportunity to gain eternal life with him.' Tithing, in its simple Biblical definition is a returning to God of a portion of the material wealth he has entrusted to us. The Tithe is returned with the motive of gratitude, not duty, and the Tither places it at the top of his personal budget. *Regardless of percentages*, people are Tithers if their giving to the Lord is (1) a definite, truly grateful share which (2) they have placed at the top of their budgets so that God comes first.

It needs to be repeated that Tithing is the right and serious way to give. Don't miss the point! Tithing is not primarily a means for raising money, nor a tax, nor a substitute for other methods for getting money to meet our church obligations. Tithing is not 'the Wells Scheme from inside the Church'. It is not a money-raising scheme at all, but a way of teaching and a means to bring us to God. There is nothing 'slick' about Tithing, nothing 'American'; indeed I was wisely rebuked for describing Tithing as American Giving. Tithing is not 'tipping' nor 'begging'; it is Christian Giving.

WHAT IS THE CHRISTIAN STANDARD OF GIVING?

The Bishop of Milwaukee commented on this in an address entitled 'Why do we only play with our religion?' given to the Diocesan Convention, and added: 'Let me emphasize with all the power at my command that it is not just money that we are concerned about. Money can be a curse, even in the Church! Some of our most richly endowed parishes are the deadest of all. I know a parish in New York that has a paid quartet from the Metropolitan Opera every Sunday, but there are no people to worship God. No, it isn't money we need; it is consecrated and dedicated souls! Men and women and children who are in earnest about their prayers, who are striving, however poorly, to seek first the Kingdom of God. . . . *It is not Tithing alone, but the complete dedication that Tithing reveals that we must seek for in our people. It hardly seems necessary to add that we cannot expect of them, the rank and file, anything that the clergy and lay leaders have not already dedicated themselves to.*' (My italics.)

Although this discussion is focussed on the Christian Giving aspect of stewardship, our Christian use of money must be thought of in larger terms than just giving, important as it is. The Christian use of money involves all our spending and anyone who regards himself as a 'steward' will never be content with any interpretation of Christian Giving which stops with the idea that we owe God a percentage. Such a limited concept misunderstands the principles of Christian Giving and actually denies that we are stewards under

God. It has been said that the law of the Tithe says 'Give 10% and enjoy the rest'. The principle of stewardship says, 'I am the servant of God placed on earth to do his will, responsible to him for all that I possess and all that I spend. It is his, not mine, even what I spend on myself is his'. Certainly no Christian can overlook the question: 'How can I spend my income so that all of it will promote the good and hinder the evil?' All this needs underlining because few people have ever considered right spending as part of Christian stewardship.

WHY DO PEOPLE DECIDE TO TITHE?

There is apparently no single answer to the question of what leads a man or woman to try this way of giving. Many are uncomfortable about old habits of giving that leave them with a feeling of spiritual emptiness. Here are some reasons people gave when they were asked what made them decide to Tithe: 'We felt we were not getting as much out of life as we should.' 'We want to express our gratitude to God.' 'We realized that in not Tithing we were not trusting God implicitly.' 'A Methodist friend told me about it.' 'The way it was explained in church.' 'The Bishop told us about it.'

But there were problems. No one goes into Tithing casually. A profound reorganization of living habits is involved—for the individual and for the family. Here is what some Americans said about their apprehensions and how it all worked out: 'I was afraid I couldn't afford it, but we managed to pay our bills and get along with plenty, thanks to God's generosity. We had a new home and many previous commitments, but as time goes on we are getting out of the woods.' 'We don't give in order to receive, but actually, the more we give the more we are blessed with.' 'The 90% now goes farther with us than 99% did before we began to Tithe.' 'I just plunged in on faith and reasoned about it afterwards. The only problem was of giving up some of the "things" which in the long run are of no importance anyway.' 'It solved all our problems in regard to budget, commitments and—best of all—Church.'

Many Tithers now smile over past attitudes. One summed it up this way: 'As long as I didn't *understand* Tithing, I would go to fantastic lengths to invent reasons why I shouldn't accept the plan and practise it.' Another said, 'Our method wasn't very scientific. We just asked ourselves how much we could give without missing it. We used the same method in tipping bellboys and waitresses.' One housewife said, 'For years my pledge was one dollar a week. I felt that this was sufficient "admission charge".' An ex-Tither is almost unheard of. Once a family has experienced the spiritual blessings of the Tithing way of life, they say 'Never again!' to the giving habits of the past. God has been placed at the centre of their lives so that he is first in their living and first in their giving.

DO PEOPLE GROW IN GRACE THROUGH TITHING?

Yes, the initial letters of the word Tithing itself can remind us that 'Trusting it to Him is no gamble'. Tithers have discovered that a personal or family budget based on Tithing goes farther— materially as well as spiritually. There is no mystery about this: the Tither usually works from a budget, and the budget brings order to his living as well as his giving. But above all, the Tithe, as a continuing expression of *daily gratitude*, brings a peace of mind and peace of soul which cannot be experienced in any other way. Tithers are not religious fanatics. They are folk like us and ours from all classes and economic groups. But they are different. So much so that they are a mystery to others who wonder material- istically, 'How can people be happier with 90% than with 100%?' They are different because their lives have been changed in a wonderful way to the point where they are actually *living* the Prayer of Thanksgiving. Why should this be? Put briefly, there are at least three reasons: (1) Tithing teaches; (2) Tithing trains; (3) Tithing transforms.

Tithing *teaches* what is important in life. With many of us per- sonal comfort, success, pleasure, are the most important things. When time, energy and money have been given to these matters, then God may have a bit of what is left. Tithing reverses this order. It recognizes a truth that can be denied or forgotten only at the peril of rendering our lives ultimately shallow: that God, not man, is the central fact around which all life revolves. Again, Tithing teaches an awareness of the presence of God. The principle behind Tithing is that every material thing—though we may call it ours—actually belongs to God. He owns it all: our property, our income, our life. This is God's world. The man who Tithes does so because he knows whose world this is. This leads to worship. For worship is the giving of self and Tithing teaches that, unworthy as we are, we may offer ourselves to God. When we are giving our money seriously, responsibly, gratefully, we are giving ourselves.

Tithing *trains* people in practical application. The Tither sees things differently. This has been a constant claim of those who have been working with American parishes. One big difference in the Tither's outlook is in how he sees his Church at every level. Here is what people said about how that had been changed: 'It makes "our" Church.' 'It has made the Church part of us.' 'Your heart follows even one-tenth of your treasure.' 'When you invest your money you want to put it to good use. I find myself impatient with ineffective leadership.' And when God's world looks different, the people in it look different too. Many Tithers said they find friendships and family ties strengthened. 'It leads towards the Christ-centred family.' 'We are more deeply rooted in God's family.' 'There's a feeling of *belonging* you can't describe.'

The chief claim made in the Diocese of Michigan is that Tithing will *transform* the Tither. As first-hand evidence that this claim is true, here is what people said about how Tithing affected them: 'I realize now that to be the right kind of Christian I must give thanks to God in a practical way.' 'It showed me the joy of knowing God.' 'I used to be distracted sometimes by the clothes of obviously wealthy people in the parish. This no longer bothers me, because I know we are now supporting our Church as well as they.' 'The real fun is in the joy of being a "rich man". I find we can now give $50 where $5 was "all we could afford" before we started Tithing.'

Answer to this query must close with an underlining of the purpose of Tithing. Don't miss the point! Tithing is a spiritual practice—'an orderly method by which God's children in God's ordered universe express their gratitude to him for all of his wonderful blessings'. Regardless of percentages, they are Tithers if their giving to God is a definite, truly grateful share which they have placed at the top of their budgets so that God comes first. The Tithe is a regular proportion for God, but it is more than simple arithmetic. The Tithe is not only a part but a symbol of a whole.

This growing in grace by individuals and by congregations will not happen suddenly. But it will happen! *After seven years of teaching* about proportionate giving, most of the congregation in one Michigan parish give 5% to the Church. Since this standard is taught and assumed, it has raised the giving of all their members. Now, two things happen. First, the PCC has real dignity and proper resources. They give to poorer parishes; they meet their diocesan responsibilities in a businesslike manner; they do not haggle all night talking about jobs, but they do them. Secondly, *and this is the great thing*, if we put this into effect, it will free the clergy and all church officers for the more fundamental matters that our Lord would have us do—the reaching of the unchurched, the quality of the Sunday school, the adult education, and the giving to new work.

One final point about the spiritual joys of Tithing. It is quoted from Bishop Emrich. 'Now, a group of able laity—God bless them —have taken this whole Tithing movement out of my hands. A talented layman wrote the pamphlet we are using in this movement. Two laymen have raised among friends enough money to adapt this pamphlet into a motion picture. Many other laymen are helping to follow it through on their parish level. I want this to be a lay movement, with convocational and parish groups that teach it all year long. I have yet to meet a serious layman who does

63

not agree that finally we are on the right track and that we will begin to accomplish something by this. It is deeply religious, business-like and serious.'

HOW TO DECIDE WHAT IS A GRATEFUL SHARE?

This is a decision which is made directly between each one of us and our Heavenly Father, 'from whom no secrets are hid'. If it were otherwise, it would contradict the whole principle of Tithing as a spiritual practice. Deciding what is a grateful share is the result of devout prayer as well as careful and reverent thinking. No one on earth can tell another person what to give. But if we will draw up a budget and ask God to guide us in deciding what is a fair share for him, he will help us find the answer. We and our families will know in our hearts if we are 'tipping' God or whether we have set aside a truly grateful share, after considering all the blessings the Lord has given each one of us. And God will know, too. When we stop to think how much of our weekly wages is spent on pleasure only, and compare that with the amount given to God, there are very few of us who can refrain from blushing with shame.

'What? Giving again?' I asked in dismay;
   'And must I keep giving and give alway?'
'Oh no,' said the Angel, whose eyes pierced me through,
   'Just stop when the Saviour stops giving to you.'[1]

HOW DO PEOPLE GET STARTED ON TITHING?

The husband and wife—or other family group—agree, in a spirit of deeply shared gratitude to God, that they would like to be Tithers. They estimate how much they can give as a *beginning* Tithe. This beginning Tithe may be less than 5%, as long as it is a definite percentage, carefully thought out and represents the return to God of a grateful proportion of what they are receiving from his bounty. They take this amount, whatever it is, and put

[1] I am unable to trace the source of this verse.

it at the top of their weekly or monthly budget, so that *God is placed first*. At every Sunday service, they offer a part of their Tithe. As they Tithe they discover the many blessings of Tithing, including the ease and simplicity with which God helps them to do it. They wish that they had discovered Tithing long before!

Most new Tithers do not begin with the full 5 and 5 percentage because it is too strenuous a jump from their pre-Tithing standard of giving. I admit that I have myself only just reached the stage of giving God 5% of my £300 p.a. The average new Tither begins with one or two or three per cent for the Church, increasing it from year to year, 'as God hath prospered him'. This is practical, and a rise in salary or the completion of a hire purchase payment are both excellent opportunities to begin Tithing. Many folk in England believe that 5% is too much for the Church to expect or to teach. But this objection is realistic only on a most superficial level. The full 5% allows folk to grow in grace while striving for it. To Tithe 1%, as is being suggested in some parishes in this country, would be easy: it would cost nothing. Christian Giving *begins* when it begins to hurt. The degree of self-deception which some of us practise at this point is amazing! Most people who do not keep accounts exaggerate the amount they are giving away. We think of the generous gifts we would give if we could 'just afford it'. Such dream-giving pays no clergy, builds no churches, sends out no missionaries, feeds no hungry, but it does enable us to put conscience to rest.

We grow in grace by giving as much as we can. There need be no exception to this principle. It is as applicable to old age pensioners as to newly-weds or to folk with variable incomes. However small our income, we should still expect to offer a definite share to God. I have analysed many collections and discovered that the highest giving per capita week by week was at Lincoln Theological College. This is the most Christian community I have encountered; it is also a community in which money is very scarce. In other words, the poorest community was giving the most money to God. One advantage of the clergy

Tithing is the example and encouragement to every one of modest means. Certainly if the junior clergy can Tithe on £5 15s. od. weekly, most members of most congregations can and ought to do likewise. There is no special virtue in Tithing at 5% and then getting so accustomed to it that it no longer 'costs'. Tithing is sacrificial. This is of far greater importance than its being systematic. We should offer God something which 'costs'. Most of us will find, however, that it 'hurts' to give the full 5 and 5 percentage (after Income Tax is deducted). This leads to several shorter considerations.

PEOPLE ASK THESE QUESTIONS ABOUT TITHING

(1) What is the difference between Tithing and Proportionate Giving? The principle of each is the same. The Modern Tithe gives us a Christian standard, but leaves the decision of what is a truly grateful share up to the giver. Proportionate Giving establishes a table of incomes for various sized families and fixes definite amounts to give.

(2) 'I do not have a fixed or definite income. How can I Tithe?' You set aside a definite, planned percentage of all that you take in. Your estimate can be based on your minimum expectations. Amounts that you set aside in addition to your estimate can be given at any time as special gifts over and above the Tithe.

(3) 'How can I give alms "in secret" if I Tithe?' Jesus said, 'Beware of practising your piety before men in order to be seen by them!' He went on to apply this to alms giving—'When you give alms do not let your left hand know what your right hand is doing, so that your alms may be in secret; and your Father who sees in secret will reward you.' (Matt. 6.3-5). Tithing is a personal decision with God. But it is well nigh impossible to do more than restrict to a minimum those who need to know the exact amount. There is a difference between spreading personal pride, which Jesus condemned, and knowledge acquired by a small number of church officials. It would seem to be wrong to use a plate rather than a bag, in the hope of larger collections, and equally wrong to

publish 'pace setting pledges'. In England, however, the greatest temptation is to allow secrecy and reticence as a cover for meanness! A church treasurer told me recently that it would be wrong to train folk to give when it hurts because they would cease to be the cheerful givers whom the Lord loves!

(4) 'What if I promised to Tithe and then find it impossible to fulfil my promise?' God understands. Tithing is not a contract. It is a Christian intention. The only contract you make is your personal pact with God to try his way of using money. This promise is revocable at any time. No parish should hold a member to it if he changes his mind. To do so would defeat the whole purpose of Tithing. There are no benefits from a Tithe that is not given of our own free will. A Church ought to make only one request to would-be Tithers: that they resolve to give it a fair trial—six months at the minimum. There are real problems in England about Tithing amidst our present economic situation. But, as an American has pointed out, it might be more fitting in our welfare state for the Church to teach a 7 and 3 percentage for Church and charity rather than the 5 and 5. If they are considered in the light of God's redeeming love, and with a view to answering the question, how much shall we give? And not, how little? then our Heavenly Father will understand and will help us.

IS IT CHRISTIAN TO TEACH ABSTRACT GIVING?

This has perplexed several people, mainly because of a quotation in my article in *Theology*—'The inner group—parochial or diocesan—must, of course, prepare a budget. *But don't go to your people with a budget.* Gratitude to God, and not the inadequate budget, should be the motive for your giving.' This raises—and answers—the question, Should congregations be trained to give without reference to a target? This whole discussion is based on the affirmative, but some find this difficult to accept. I think of Christian Giving as a spiritual practice similar to prayer. The basis of both is the same, namely, self-offering. And intercession is primarily an entering into the love of God and subsequently a bringing to God. How wise are the words from Lady Julian's Revelation of Divine Love: 'And in this he brought to mind the property of a glad giver. A glad giver taketh but little heed of the thing that he giveth, but all his desire and all his intent is to please him and to solace him to whom he giveth it' (9th Revelation, Ch. 23). It should not perplex a Christian not to know church uses for his money in advance any more than it worries him not to know for whom his intercessions will be desired soon.

There is, of course, a need for the PCC and congregation to discuss and accept a budget either tentatively subject to review after pledges are received, or, after pledges are in, the budget should be worked out. This is in order that members of the congregation may participate in the planning and carrying out of their own financial programme. In some parishes in England the members are not enough involved in their own planning. The budget is too cut-and-dried, worked out by the vicar and wardens, and just announced to the congregation. There is a real need for the *whole* congregation to face the question, What goes to the top of the parish budget? its own needs or the spread of Christ's Kingdom? And in many parishes there is at present no budget at all.

WHAT ABOUT BAZAARS AND SALES OF WORK?

These are unworthy ways of raising money to meet *normal financial responsibilities*. This statement may contradict established traditions up and down the country: it does not alter the fact that sales of work are sub-Christian as *a means of alms-giving*. They are fund-raising ideas, but there seems to be no theological or spiritual basis for them as proper means of Christian Giving. This needs clarification—though surely not modification! If a Christian community depends on bazaars for a large proportion of its income year by year, such a community has failed to understand that Christian Giving is a spiritual practice. Many parishes rely on their bazaars for vital funds, and run them very successfully. Nevertheless, such dependence can only be described as sub-Christian by anyone who has the courage to think out Christian Giving. The Bible says a great deal about Christian Giving: it says nothing at all about bazaars, sales of work, 'tipping' or 'begging' as ways of returning a grateful share to God. I have not written that bazaars are wrong. They are not. The giving of time and the giving of ability are just as important as alms-giving. Stewardship involves all our giving. But what is wrong is *the utter dependence on bazaars as a substitute for alms-giving*. These activities have great value as social occasions and as opportunities for people to use their creative talents in a true spirit of stewardship. But even granting these genuine benefits, I have often wondered what God could do with all the energy we have to mobilize for these occasions. (I well remember my first month in parish life. There were jumble sales every Saturday. The purpose was to raise funds to stock the stalls at the Christmas Sale. The absence of real training in Christian Giving is driving many parishes to hold pre-sale sales, to raise money to raise money.) If only this energy could be dedicated to evangelism instead of fund-raising! As fund-raising concerns, bazaars should be limited to special financial requirements or emergencies over and above the normal. Thus, from the standpoint of Christian Giving, it would be proper to have a sale of work to support Hungarian refugees or meet some similar emergency. It would be wrong to rely on an annual sale of work in order to meet, say, annual missionary obligations. The vastness of bazaars and sales of work raising large sums throughout the land has never justified the principles on which they are based. There is no substitute for Christian Giving. And if we did not have to waste so much time flapping about these bazaars, we would appreciate this a great deal sooner and get on with spreading the Gospel.

IS CHRISTIAN GIVING AN ACT OF WORSHIP?

It should be. 'Giving is an act of worship' was one of the American slogans which first persuaded me that they had something to teach us. In the Church of England at the vast majority of services the plate or bag is shuffled round and presented at the altar during a hymn.[1] Is this an act of congregational *worship*? What is the effect on an untrained congregation? One remedy is a pause during the hymn so that attention can be concentrated on the presentation of our offering while the officiant says 'Accept, O Lord, these gifts, for all things come of thee and of thine own have we given thee'. But even this becomes automatic if it is not explained frequently. It is significant that a collection is specifically appointed only at the Holy Communion; but there is a danger that the Offertory procession can swing the emphasis away from the offering of our money. Giving is an act of worship only where this is explained and appreciated; otherwise it is difficult to give our offering a meaningful place in services of worship.

WHAT DOES THE BIBLE TEACH ABOUT CHRISTIAN GIVING?

A detailed analysis is beyond the scope of this discussion.[2] It is a valuable exercise—surely a 'must'—for clergy and lay folk to discover for themselves what the Bible teaches about Christian Giving. Someone told me recently that there was hardly sufficient about Giving in the Bible for a single sermon or Bible study. Yet it is surprising to find how much our Lord has to say about this subject. Principal Denney is reported to have declared that more is said about money in the New Testament than about anything else. It is interesting that although we do not know a great deal about routine duties amongst the Twelve we are informed that they had a treasurer.

In Gen. 28.22, Jacob said to God 'And of all that thou givest me I will give the tenth to thee', and throughout Old Testament history one-tenth was the portion set aside by religious law as God's

---

[1] In the Free Churches matters are differently and more responsibly handled; no doubt partly because few Free Churches have much in the way of endowments.

[2] *Christian Giving*, by V. S. Azariah, late Bishop of Dornakal in South India (World Christian Books, Lutterworth Press, 2s. 6d.) is an admirable statement of the theology of Christian Giving.

share. Some of the Old Testament gifts were obligatory, some voluntary. An example of the former is the Tithe (Lev. 27.30-2), and of the latter the gifts for the Tabernacle (Ex. 25.2). In the case of some of the offerings the cost was graded to make allowance for the poor, but everyone was expected to give something. Taken altogether, devout Hebrews must have given about a third of their income. These gifts were offered to God. 'Speak to the children of Israel, that they take for me an offering: from every man whose heart makes him willing you shall receive the offering for me' (Ex. 25.2).

A close study of Old Testament texts, especially in the original, reveals Hebrew attitudes which are unexpected. It is tempting to equate Judaism with legalism and thus to assume that Old Testament giving is exclusively legal. A first glance at Tithing gives the impression that this is nothing but a system, a requirement by religious law. But the principle of Tithing was established long before the giving of the Law, and it was carefully formulated and regulated in the Law. Abraham was not under the Law, nor was Jacob—the Law simply embodied a principle already established. Hebrew thought is not confined to the legal aspects: it is possible to trace some realization that Giving is a spiritual practice, springing from a right relationship with God. Deut. 16 contains instructions about attendance at appointed feasts, adding, 'They shall not appear before the Lord empty-handed; every man shall give as he is able according to the blessing of the Lord your God which he has given you'. These words are a summary of the previous verses and, indeed, of the biblical idea of gratitude. This is more obvious in the Hebrew: a literal translation of the first half is 'They shall not allow themselves to be seen before the face of God in an empty condition'. The word for 'empty-handed' is difficult to render. It means emptily, vainly, worthless, in an empty condition. And behind this seems to be the Hebrew realization that they were ever in God's sight and that they should not appear empty but grateful. In this chapter this realization is given specific reference and context, but the principles behind it are the principles of everyday life in relation to God. The Hebrews recognized that Giving was also a privilege which brought joy and blessing.

Malachi has a very pertinent cry: 'Will man rob God? Yet you are robbing me. But you say, How are we robbing Thee? In your Tithes and offerings. You are cursed with a curse, for you are robbing me; the whole nation of you. Bring the full Tithes into the storehouse, that there may be food in my house; and thereby put me to the test, says the Lord of hosts, if I will not open the windows of heaven for you and pour down for you an overflowing blessing' (Mal. 3.8-10).

There is more in the Gospels, said Bishop Gore, against being rich and in favour of being poor than most of us like to recognize. This is not peculiar to any one Gospel. We cannot explain away the sternness of our Lord's teaching. It has been well said that 'The tendency of most of us to soften down our Lord's uncompromising words to ease the pressure on our own consciences is just one more illustration of that "deceitfulness of riches" upon which he insisted.' There is no doubt about what Jesus said (Matt. 19.23-26; Mark 10.23-5; Luke 18.24-5). Our Lord warned men that even alms-giving might be robbed of any spiritual value if it be done for show (cf. Mark 10.21; Luke 6.30; 12.33). A service rendered in expectation of a return gift is no gift (Luke 14.12-14). Jesus did not say that great possessions are sinful, but that they are dangerous. There is no hint in the Parables of the Talents or the Unjust Steward, which deal with the use of money, that Jesus disapproved of its possession, although they stress the fundamental importance of its right employment. No one thinks of money as an end in itself: it is always a means. The real question is, A means to what? Our Lord's answer is that money should be a means to seeking the Kingdom of God and his righteousness. It is in the light of this master principle that all the issues must be considered. Christian Giving, like the Christian use of money in general, must be an expression of an attitude of life.

'For you know the grace of our Lord, Jesus Christ, that though he was rich, yet for your sake he became poor, so that by his poverty you might become rich' (II Cor. 8.9). Here is the inspiration of our Christian Giving and St Paul gives much wise guidance to his congregations. There is no finer writing on this subject than in the great chapters in II Corinthians. But perhaps the most quoted words are: 'Upon the first day of the week let everyone of you lay by him in store, as the Lord has prospered him' (I Cor. 16.2). It is interesting to note that Paul issued these instructions in order to avoid the necessity of a special fund-raising effort. He goes on to say in the concluding words of the sentence: 'that there be no gatherings when I come.' Many members of the Church at Corinth must have lived very close to the poverty line. Paul did not ask that specific commitments be made. He asked that Christians used the first day of the week as a time for examining their financial responsibility to brethren who were suffering. In II Corinthians Paul tells how the Philippians gave and how he expected the Corinthians to give also. In these chapters we can trace all the principles of Christian Giving—joyful, sacrificial, whole-hearted, generous, purposeful. Both Jesus and Paul emphasize that stewards have responsibilities to members of their own families. The New Testament makes this very clear. In Mark 9.7f. Jesus rebuked those who claimed that a vow given to God absolved them from their responsibility to father and mother. Paul says, 'If anyone does not provide for his relatives, and especially for his own family, he has disowned the faith and is worse than an unbeliever' (I Tim. 5.8). This needs to be stated in spite of the fact that there are those who use the need for charity at home as an excuse for not practising charity away from home. The story of the Widow's Mite is not only central in our Lord's teaching, but specially relevant in these days when many of the community face financial hardship. Jesus said: 'Truly I say to you, this poor widow has put in more than all those who are contributing to the treasury. For they all contributed out of their abundance; but she out of her poverty has put in everything she had, her whole living' (Mark 12.43). There are many 'poor widows' in our congregations to-day and they put us to shame. To those who contribute out of their abundance, there is no more challenging question than: does—

> Love so amazing, so divine,
> Demand my soul, my life—and sixpence?

The Bible states clearly that our desire for possessions must be kept in line with the will of God. This section has listed some of the passages which say how we as Christians should be guided in our use of God's gifts. The needs of our neighbours must take priority over our desire for something we can in fact do without. So also must the needs of the Church for money to carry forward its work of preaching and reaching. The Offertory Sentences provide rich material for meditation and preaching on the biblical basis for Christian Giving.

THE WAY AHEAD

THE previous section did not provide all the answers to Christian Giving on this side of the Atlantic. Indeed anyone who claimed to know all the answers to this problem would succeed only in revealing his ignorance and inexperience. I will never know enough about this aspect of Christian life, but I did see how dioceses and parishes of every size and condition *were transformed* by seeking first the principles of Christian Giving. Nothing in this discussion is imaginary or theoretical. Real evidence is offered to provoke thought and prayer and action, but no slick answers. It can be criticized by folk who know better or who have done differently. Perhaps chief among these will be those who are content to go on raising money by successful raffles and bazaars and by those whose parishes have experienced real blessings through 'vocational technicians' as one fund-raising firm calls its staff.

This possibility leads back to two significant omissions from the previous section: (1) what proof is there that this will work here? and (2) how I personally would try to use Christian Giving on a parish level.

WILL IT WORK HERE?

(1) Christian Giving in this country requires faith more than proof. Certainly I have no list of parishes which have "proved" that Christian Giving is part of the Christian life. Proofs of successful bazaars or campaigns bettering their targets are no substitute for thinking out the principles and then planning parish action in accord with these principles and with local requirements. In some quarters it is suggested that there is no substitute for

experience in fund-raising. But I must confess my belief that the proper basis for all experiments in Christian Giving must be faith plus experience. It is not true—though it is widely believed in England—that fund-raising firms are the only people to 'prove' anything about Christian Giving. 'The need of the giver to give' was a New Testament truth long before it became a professional slogan. Nevertheless, I must be explicit at this point and emphasize that this reporter is a young man, only recently ordained; he has not conducted any successful campaigns! But the truth of a report does not depend on the age of the writer but on accurate and honest discussion of authentic evidence.

But some of my older friends press for proof. For the benefit of those who want proof, I may reproduce here a letter from *Theology* for November 1957, and a report which appeared in *The Times* on May 7th, 1958.

Dear Sir,

It is quite possible for 'Modern Tithing', as described by Mr Rice in your September number, to operate in England as well as in America; and I would say that here, too, we can best tackle Christian Giving from the inside. A Direct Giving Campaign, run in the Bishop of Michigan's words with 'gratitude to God and not the inadequate budget' as the motive of giving, can become a powerful handle of mission and, incidentally, transform the annual income of a church. This parish ran a Direct Giving (or 'Modern Tithing') Campaign earlier in the year with John 3.16 as the running theme. Many people found that they were faced afresh with the question, 'What think ye of Christ?' In hard cash this campaign has meant that a weekly income which a year ago was under £6 has now become one of over £60. If Christian Giving is to become the naturally accepted responsibility of the people of the Church, there is need, as Mr Rice emphasized, for continued teaching about it.

One further point of agreement with the author of the article—All Souls', Ancoats, is not patronized by millionaires.

It is in the English scene like the church Mr Rice referred to in the American, a workers' church in an industrial area.

Yours faithfully,

J. B. R. GRINDROD

All Souls' Rectory,
Ancoats, Manchester 4

This is a fine and encouraging situation, and needs to be pondered. What is of the greatest significance is that the giving in this working-class parish has increased at so striking a rate entirely through the people's response to God's demand as they came to understand it. This is proof; and it was obtained by the vicar (who had been in the parish well under a year at the time) and congregation going forward in faith. Equally instructive is the experience of Birmingham Parish Church; and it may be noted that though the fundamental principles are those for which I have been arguing, their practical application offers yet another variation—further evidence of the general validity of the Gospel principles and their practical adaptability to the circumstances of a particular congregation.

A TENTH FOR CHARITY
PARISH SCHEME FOR DIRECT GIVING
From Our Own Correspondent

Birmingham, May 6th

Members of the congregation of St Martin's-in-the-Bullring, the parish church of Birmingham, have agreed to devote a tenth of their disposable income—the Old Testament tithe—to charity, including church funds. Canon Bryan Green, the rector, says this will raise the direct income of St Martin's from £5,500 to £8,000 a year and enable them to dispense with collections and appeals.

Canon Green freely acknowledges that the Birmingham scheme owes much in concept to methods of direct giving by which many American churches raise funds. He knows of some

77

25 churches in Britain that have called in professional appeal organizing firms to raise funds, but he believes St Martin's is the first to organize a comprehensive scheme from within its own resources.

A team of laymen is being led by a professional accountant in the congregation who has been released by his firm to launch the appeal. Members are being asked to calculate their annual net income after meeting the essential commitments of modern living. The church is not attempting an exhaustive definition of these liabilities but suggests as guidance such items as income tax, rates, rents, mortgage repayments, insurance and superannuation contributions.

From the residual income the individual is asked to set aside a tenth for what Canon Green calls 'general benevolence'. A proportion left to each member to decide for himself will go to the church (by way of a three-year pledge, it is suggested, to allow the church to plan its use), the remainder to other charities and good works.

Shock to Members

If the scheme were accepted by every parish in England it would 'revolutionize the finances of the Church of England', Canon Green said. Much of the extra income St Martin's will derive from the scheme is to be given away. 'To give away money is a healthy thing for the Church to do. We should not always be asking,' he added.

Most members of the church, he said, received a shock when they worked out the financial implications of the scheme. Many found they had been giving away far less of their money than a Christian ought. A few were already giving away more than they would be asked to do under the scheme. Individual weekly contributions already pledged to St Martin's range from 3d. (from children) to £2.

The direct giving is only part of a wider scheme planned by St Martin's to enlist the laity in the wider life of the Church.

PRACTICAL SUGGESTIONS

(2) I have learned much from the guidance and experience of others about starting Christian Giving in the parish. No two parishes are alike, but the same principles can form the basis of operations anywhere. It is not until we have mastered the basic principles that we can begin to adapt their use to our own needs and our own styles. After all, the fundamental concern is not what the Americans (or Birmingham, or Manchester) are doing, but how we can practise Christian Giving in our parishes; nor is it what success we have but whether we are on the right lines. I think Christian Giving could be developed along the following lines, even in parishes which receive little help or guidance from the diocese.

I. The clergy and their families have to Tithe, not as pace-setters, but because there is no other way to understand Christian Giving.

II. Parish strategy has to be thought out in long-term planning. It has taken Michigan parishes seven years to get into full stride, even with diocesan backing. There will rarely be overnight success. It takes time to educate ourselves into new habits of Giving.

III. Clergy who are prepared to think along these lines, then have to launch their ideas from the inside, beginning with themselves. A sudden burst of power-preaching to a bewildered congregation does not work. Instead, Christian Giving needs careful and patient preparation, first of the Finance Committee (if this exists), then of the Parochial Church Council, and finally of the Sunday school staff, and officials from all parish groups. Often a Tithing Commission, with a representative from every parish group, will need to be formed as a sub-committee of the PCC. It is important for the clergy to hand over control to the laity at the earliest possible moment, and then remain in the background as resource leaders.

IV. Little progress can be made until all these *inner groups* fully understand Tithing and are prepared to back it for a trial of at least one year. It may take years to work up a parish to this stage. Even in the most active parishes, the ideal would probably be to start preparing quietly in September and to launch Tithing on the congregation as part of the Lenten exercises. If Tithing received initial support from the inner circles, it should be possible to train a small team of visitors to call on members of the congregation during Lent. It would be of little use to push the faithful into this project until they had been properly instructed in visiting. These visitors could encourage those who did not begin Tithing as a Lenten discipline, to try it as part of their response to Good Friday and Easter Day. These visits should be restricted to homes of members of the congregation: no begging from outsiders is required.

V. When the parish officers understand Tithing and are prepared to back it by their own Tithes and encouragement, it is possible to awaken parochial interest on all levels—by sermons, by the parish magazine, by teaching in Sunday school and Confirmation instruction, by special literature, and, above all, by personal contacts. This has to continue all the year round every year. Even in the smallest parish, the inner groups will yield at least a dozen missionaries for the idea.

VI. The way the money is given will vary. It should be weekly and personally related to personal religion and Sunday worship. Annual cheques or Banker's Orders are ideal for club subscriptions, but not for acts of worship. In some parishes an envelope scheme will help; in others it will not. Some parishes may use 'Tithe-cards', so that folk may make definite commitments. At all events, it should be a combination of the two great American maxims: 'Giving is an Act of Worship' and 'I expect my church to use sound business practices'.

VII. At the present time the Extension Committee of the Central Board of Finance is only at the beginning of its work. This means that much will at first have to be done by individual parishes. This is an important weakness for two reasons:[1]

---

[1] But it would not be impossible to get started on such a basis.

1. There is a 'morale' element for parishes and PCCs if they realize that others are engaged in the same venture, in fact, pioneering adventure.

2. There is an important source of strength and 'professional' knowledge in having a group of parishes undertaking the planning, preparation of literature, visual-aid material, and so on. No one English parish is likely to have 'experts' in all promotional fields, and some might not have any. The recruiting of laymen to undertake such work would be facilitated if they had the feeling that their 'expertize' would benefit other parishes than merely their local one.

This leads me to suggest that until such time as diocesan and national Church boards have made more progress in pushing Christian Giving, it might be useful to organize—beginning with only a few parishes—a 'Fellowship of Tithing Churches,' similar to the one in the Presbyterian Church, USA. The Presbyterians had no 'diocesan' or national agency to promote their programme so devised the system of small groups of churches pioneering and co-operating together.

There is no single blue-print on Christian Giving which can be speedily applied in any one of a thousand or more parishes. Every parish has its own peculiarities, background and special difficulties. But a common feature is that we face financial difficulties at almost every level of church life. Most parishes have this in common, if nothing else. Perhaps the comparison ends here, since there is no one way to put over Christian Giving in the parish. The lines along which I personally feel that Christian Giving should be developed will doubtless not commend themselves in every parish. They are not offered with this intention. They are offered as setting down the principles of Christian Giving so that we may use these as the right basis for working this out in individual parishes and dioceses.

Those who are inclined to reject American evidence and to doubt the suggestions about application will be harder put to deny the principles from which the evidence and suggestions have sprung. The evidence and suggestions may be discounted by the reader, yet if they have provoked him to think out Christian Giving for himself and how to spread it in his own parish, then this discussion will have served its purpose. If we can share principles and experiments with our American brethren and work them out in our own parishes, we shall surely move further along the way of dedicated Christian living and towards parish churches which are capable of reaching beyond their congregations.

I. A CRITIQUE OF PROFESSIONAL
FUND-RAISING

THERE is a real place in church work for money-raising firms. They have been a great success in many parts of the world. At the moment the Diocese of Michigan needs one and a half million dollars for essential building purposes. The drive is being conducted by an outside firm. Again, the parish in which I serve needs a lot of money quickly and is considering professional assistance. There may be no alternative in this particular situation. There may be no other way to raise money quickly. A professional firm brings considerable experience and 'know-how' which our parish does not possess. We need money quickly—the beetle was discovered in the church last year; our church school is in such a dangerous condition that it has been evacuated; the church lighting needs restoration, and so on. We need hundreds of pounds quickly. And one way for our parish to meet its immediate commitments is by employing professional assistance. I do not know how we can raise the money without this assistance. This is true of many parishes. The most effective way of *target-raising* is by employing an outside firm.

Nothing in the above paragraph is intended to contradict the line taken in the main discussion. I believe firmly that at the present time there is a real place for money-raising firms. I also believe that there is a difference between target-raising and Christian Giving. It depends on the needs of each parish. If a parish needs money fast, call in professional assistance. *But if a parish needs training in Christian Giving, there is no need of outside business companies.* If the Church is getting at the real heart of this problem and teaching its members about Christian Giving as a *spiritual* practice, there should be no need of outside firms. Surely the success of fund-raising firms is possible *only* because of the failure of the Church. I have yet to hear of a parish which has been taught Christian Giving as an integral part of Christian living, needing to employ 'vocational technicians'. It is difficult to imagine a parish in which Christian Giving is systematically taught all the year round, ever having to resort to target-raising. A wise critic of my article in *Theology* has pointed out that by no means all the systems used by the American Church do credit to the Church: they may raise vast sums, but the principles are not always the worthiest.

Professional firms have a real and proper function in target-raising. But we would surely be fooling ourselves if we think that this is training people in any Christian virtue of Giving. Parishes do employ professional assistance to raise money to improve their own church, their own school, their own facilities and so on. It is not difficult to persuade people of their need to give for these purposes. It is right and necessary. But let us recognize this as target-raising for our own benefit. It is surely impossible to train a congregation to give when it hurts while the giving is mainly for improving its own facilities. I am not sure how much target-raising '*costs*' the congregation. A recent letter in a church newspaper raises the same query.

Sir,

An average weekly collection of £95 may sound wonderful, but if one analyses the figures it appears disgraceful, not wonderful.

We were informed that six hundred families promised the sum of £15,232 10s. over a three-year period, or £5,077 10s. in one year. This represents 3s. 4d. per week from each family. As a family normally consists of at least two adults this amounts to 1s. 8d. a head which is less than the cost of a packet of cigarettes or a cinema seat. Can such a paltry sum of money be described as Christian giving?

The Churches in North America have much more experience of professional firms than we have in England. So it is helpful to conclude with the considered opinions of a Canadian observer discussing the question of entering into an agreement with a fund-raising firm.

'The argument in favour of such an agreement is that the professionals know their business. When a congregation wants to build a church it hires a skilled architect. When its lighting, heating or plumbing facilities need attention, professional help is called for. There is a slight inaccuracy in the comparison, however, for architects and tradesmen are dealing with inert materials, whereas fund-raisers are dealing with people; people, moreover, whose stewardship, faith and commitment are the church's business.

The value of expert advice and help in the direction of a church fund-raising programme is not questioned. Sector plan leaders, denominational stewardship conveners, etc., are giving valuable guidance in this respect. So long as they are ministering within the communion and fellowship of the Church, subject to its appointment, its policies and jurisdiction, and motivated according to the ethic and ideals as well as inspired by the faith by which the Church lives, they must be recognized and encouraged. But this is a very different thing than hiring the services of experts who are professionals in the strict sense of that word, that is, perform for pay. These rewards, incidentally, must be substantial if one may judge not simply by the fees which are charged but also by the expansion and multiplication of fund-raising groups.

The Churches may be grateful to the professional fund-raisers for making it painfully clear that our stewardship has often been expressed in shabby terms. They have uncovered potential resources which were hitherto unknown. They have reminded us that "the children of this world are in their generation wiser than the children of light". But churchmen must surely give prayerful thought to the advisability of relinquishing to private professionals control over one of the keystones of discipleship, the stewardship of money. Let the Church, whose chief corner-stone is Jesus Christ, be faithful to its trust, exercising its full right and responsibility, retaining for itself the high privilege of teaching its children self-surrender and gratitude for the unspeakable gift of God's love. Let the Church be the Church!'[1]

[1] Quoted from *The Anglican Outlook*, March 1958, 'Professional Fund-Raising Programmes for Churches', by J. Arthur Boorman.

II. THE CONDUCT OF THE EVERY MEMBER CANVASS

THE Every Member Canvass needs careful consideration. The American version of it may not meet the needs of English parishes—but nor will any modification of it until we have studied the original. Reference should be made to Bishop Emrich's critique on pp. 43f. If anyone reads this section feeling that the Canvass experiment sounds more and more remote from our English scene, he can draw comfort and faith from the fact that many Australian clergy thought likewise—until the Every Member Canvass began revolutionizing Australian parishes.

There are now two major Canvass movements—the Every Member Canvass and the United Church Canvass. In the Every Member Canvass the local church operates as a single unit. The United Church Canvass is an interdenominational approach towards Christian Stewardship. Several congregations run a canvass simultaneously and co-ordinate their programmes. It has worked very successfully in widely differing communities in America. Among the blessings and benefits experienced through the United Church Canvass are:

1. It enriches the spiritual life through a practical programme of Christian Stewardship.
2. It saves money through wholesale buying of canvass materials.
3. It strengthens the spirit of inter-church co-operation.
4. It adds power to every participating church.
5. All churches benefit from the experience of the most successful ones.
6. Community-wide publicity strengthens the morale of all canvass workers.

87

Both canvass movements work along the same lines and they should be studied in conjunction with the two charts at the end of this section. The time schedule has been prepared with great care and wide experience has shown that changes will introduce unforeseen difficulties which greatly reduce the effectiveness of the entire canvass programme.

Experience has repeatedly shown that one of the surest ways to achieve a successful EMC is to begin working at an early date. The rector chooses a General Chairman—he needs to be a practising Christian steward and an able executive—and together they should select the chairmen of the various committees. The General Committee is called so that the Chairman can give a brief outline of the entire canvass programme, indicating the particular responsibilities of each of the committees. Immediately following this meeting, the Prospects Committee should begin assembling names for the list of pledge prospects. In its finished form this list is required at the next meeting of the General Committee, on Monday of week 1.

The task of programme building, and of interpreting it to the congregation, is made easier if it is not treated as a single whole. It has been found helpful to divide the Church's programme into five major divisions:

1. Our World Mission.
2. Our Pastoral Ministry.
3. Our Worship and Service.
4. Our Christian Education.
5. Our Church Home.

These five divisions are further sub-divided and the comprehensive programme mimeographed with every item classified under 'What we are doing' and 'What we should do'. Americans find it helpful to look first at what is already being accomplished. Great care must be exercised, however, lest this encourage the 'As it was in the beginning, is now and ever shall be' complacency.

The Survey Committee estimates the giving potential of the

parish. This was Jesus' own teaching. 'Which of you,' he asked, 'desiring to build a tower does not first sit down and count the cost, whether he have wherewith to complete it? Lest haply, when he hath laid a foundation, and is not able to finish, all that behold begin to mock him' (Luke 14.28-9). The giving potential of a parish can be estimated in many ways. The following is one of the best (in America):

1. Multiply the number of resident members by $70.[1]
2. Multiply the average Sunday attendance by 2 × $70.
3. Add 20% to the current budget of the parish.

The highest of these three amounts is a reasonable figure on which to base a parish programme for the New Year. When the Survey Committee Chairman has finally secured the figure for the estimated giving potential, he meets with the Programme Chairman, on Tuesday of week 4, and the final programme is prepared for presentation to church members at the Congregational Dinner Meeting of Tuesday of week 5.

The major task of the Education Committee is to interpret the proposals made by the Programme Committee. This can be done in a number of ways—lay testimonials on the value of Stewardship are very effective; brief leaflets describing aspects of Stewardship are available (even in England); securing a large attendance for the Dinner Meeting (a return postcard should be included with the letter of invitation, and the ' 'phone squad' should be alerted).

The Prospects Committee gathers the names and addresses of all pledge-prospects. This task is one which cannot be done quickly. Great care is needed about motives in compiling this list. 'Begging from outsiders' may bring in more money, but this is not Christian Giving. Here the difference between target-raising and Christian Giving is involved and this will receive further consideration later.

The Publicity Committee prepare various letters. Publicity needs the greatest consideration and care in England. Inferior

[1] The national average weekly wage at the time was approximately $75.

publicity based on dull and unimaginative literature will never commend the Gospel to the present generation. The American Churches have been very quick to move with the times in this respect. The publications teaching Christian Giving to children are excellent. Usually the Publicity Committee function more by mail and telephone than by posters. Usually a lady is chosen to head the ' 'phone squad'. Six letters are sent out normally. The form below is for letter 1. It has been used effectively and can be readily adapted to the needs of any parish:

Dear friend:

A week from next Tuesday evening, our church will have a Congregational Dinner Meeting. The purpose will be to consider plans for an enlarged programme for our church in the new year. I think you will be pleased when you hear about the plans to make our church a more effective witness for Christ in our community.

We want you to be present to share your views. The plans which will be presented are only tentative. They will be freely discussed. And we invite you to make suggestions for a more effective programme to be adopted as our goal for the coming year.

Please return the enclosed card promptly, reserving your place at the dinner, which will be served at six-thirty.

Sincerely,

———

General Chairman, EMC.

PS. Arrangements have been made for the care of small children during the meeting time.

The provision of needed supplies at the right time for all committees is the responsibility of the Materials Committee. In America all supplies are available from the Joint Department of Stewardship and Benevolence in New York.

The Visitations Chairman should be the kind of person with whom others are pleased to work, who is accustomed to detailed procedures and who can be depended upon to continue a job until it is finished. The success of the entire canvass programme will depend largely on the effectiveness with which the canvassers do their work on Stewardship Sunday. The number of canvassers needed will be about a quarter of the number of homes represented on the master list. Then, as they go forth, two by two, each team will be asked to make only six calls. These they probably can complete between 2 and 6 p.m. on Stewardship Sunday. Besides Canvassers, Captains (over four teams) will be needed, and in parishes with more than 500 members, Division Leaders (over four Captains) should also be chosen.

The vital point is not enlisting, but *training* the canvassers. The Church in the modern world has rarely made any progress by sending out untrained lay people. Every effort should be put forth to prepare them to do their job well. No one goes out to 'preach' what he has not himself practised. There are many experiments in the use of training sessions. They narrow down to the formula that each rector and General Chairman must find the appropriate way to put over Stewardship in their parish. There are many ways of training and they all stem from personal example. Christian Giving is widespread in America because many of the clergy know what it means to give until it hurts. Our English clergy ask how they can get their people started on Christian Giving, the answer is 'If *you* started to give until it hurts, you will know how to guide others'. This has been condemned as a 'slick answer'; but no one has challenged its truth.

On Stewardship Sunday the morning service is of such significance that unusual efforts are put forth to insure the largest possible attendance. Reminder cards and telephone calls contact every family on the master list. After a sermon on Stewardship the vicar makes a brief statement regarding the visitation in the afternoon. Everyone is requested to remain at home till the Canvassers have called. Then the Canvassers come to the front of the church for short commissioning. They eat lunch together and then go forth. They report back in the evening with all completed pledge cards, whether they represent a pledge or a refusal. Every possible effort is put forth to complete all calls during the week so every person can enjoy the privilege of sharing in the service on Dedication Sunday, week 10.

The Dedication Sunday Service will be the climax of the whole canvass programme. When the members and friends of the parish signed their pledge cards on Stewardship Sunday, each one retained a Dedication Card for use as part of a service of dedication. The rector begins the Dedication Service by saying: 'Here in my hand I hold my pledge to our church for the year ahead. I pledge to Christ, and to you, my time, my talents, and this measure of my material possessions. As a token of this dedication, I now place this pledge on the altar.' Then representatives of the parish step forward and make appropriate dedications, and all members of the congregation bring their Dedication Cards and place them on the altar. Weekly contribution envelopes for the new year should be ready for distribution at the conclusion of the service.

After the canvass, a letter of appreciation is mailed on Tuesday of week 9 to each individual who has made a pledge. It should contain a confirmation of the amount pledged. It is important that regular reports of accomplishment should be sent to every family or person who pledge. When new members are received, their stewardship responsibilities should be explained to them without delay.

In order that members of the congregation may be kept informed of the financial status of their parish programme, a brief statement should be inserted in the magazine each month. It is best put in a box, always in the same place. Many parishes have found the following form satisfactory for this purpose:

> Our budget for the year . . . . .
> The portion for each week . . . . .
> Budget receipts for last week . . . .
> Total requirements to last Sunday . . . .
> Total receipts to last Sunday . . . .
> To bring us up to date we need . . . .

EVERY MEMBER CANVASS TIME SCHEDULE

WK	SUNDAY	MONDAY	TUESDAY	WEDNES-DAY	THURSDAY	FRIDAY	SATURDAY
1		General Committee meets	Supplies ordered	Enlist District leaders in churches over 500			
2		Photographer engaged District Leader begins enlisting captains	Programme Committee— first meeting		*Before Week I* 1. Rector chooses General Chairman 2. General Chairman chooses Committee Chairmen 3. First Meeting of General Committee 4. Prospects Committee makes Master List		
3	Photos taken	Captains begin enlisting canvassers	Group Programme Committees meet	Mail No.1 letter— Half-tones ordered			
4	Bulletin announces cong'l dinner		Programme and survey chairmen meet together	Pledge cards ordered	Telephone unaccepted cong'l meeting invitations		Enlist canvassers deadline
5	Bulletin announces cong'l dinner meeting		**Congregational Dinner Meeting**	Proposed budget half-tones to printers get pledge cards	Materials chairman begins filling in pledge cards		Hang E.M.C. posters
6	Layman speaks Captains take turnover-charts materials	Canvassers make turnover-charts				Printer delivers printed appeal folder	Letters No. 2 and No. 3 appeal folders put in envelopes
7	Layman speaks announce stewardship dedication Sundays	Mail No. 2 Letter	Mail No. 3 letter enclosing appeal folder		Telephone remind canvassers I training session		Reminder cards addressed Mail No. 4 letter
8	**Layman speaks canvassers I training session**	Mail No. 5 letter	Completed pledge cards to visitation chairman	Mail reminder cards	Telephone remind canvassers II training session	**Canvassers II training session**	Telephone call all stewardship Sunday attendance
9	**Stewardship Sunday report meeting 8 p.m.**		Mail No. 6 letter				
10	**Dedication Sunday**						

EVERY MEMBER CANVASS ORGANIZATION CHART

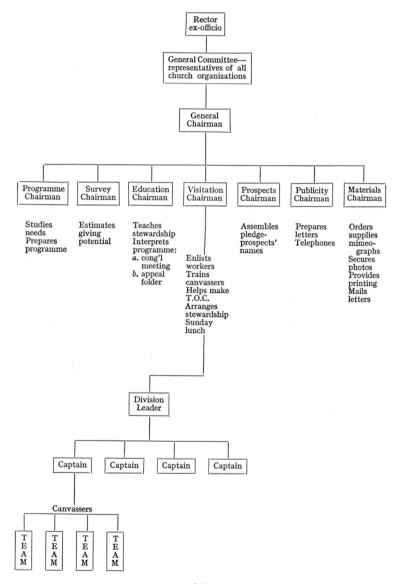

Rector
ex-officio

General Committee—
representatives of all
church organizations

General
Chairman

Programme Chairman	Survey Chairman	Education Chairman	Visitation Chairman	Prospects Chairman	Publicity Chairman	Materials Chairman
Studies needs Prepares programme	Estimates giving potential	Teaches stewardship Interprets programme: *a.* cong'l meeting *b.* appeal folder	Enlists workers Trains canvassers Helps make T.O.C. Arranges stewardship Sunday lunch	Assembles pledge-prospects' names	Prepares letters Telephones	Orders supplies mimeographs Secures photos Provides printing Mails letters

Division
Leader

Captain	Captain	Captain	Captain

Canvassers

T E A M	T E A M	T E A M	T E A M

94

III. THE COVENANT SCHEME

THE Covenant Scheme, whereby the PCC can reclaim income tax from the Chief Inspector of Taxes on gifts covenanted for seven years, has many advantages. As an example, a contribution of 2s. 6d. per week will give the parish church £6 10s. per annum plus £4 16s. 1d. in recovered tax. This has the effect, at present rates of Income Tax, of practically doubling the amount received by the church and in most cases involves no extra cost to the covenanter. The State specifically makes provision that that portion of our income which we contribute to our church or to a recognized charity be considered, in certain circumstances, to be free of Income Tax. The certain circumstances, briefly, are that a seven-year Deed of Covenant is signed, and that the tax which we have paid on the sum covered by the Deed of Covenant is recovered by the church or charity for its own use. It needs to be understood that these are only concessions on the part of the Revenue authorities. The Inspector of Taxes, Charity Division, Seafield House, Waterloo Road, Seaforth, Liverpool 21, is generally most helpful in all matters relating to Deeds of Covenant.

Difficulties arise with Covenants signed by people not paying Income Tax at the full standard rate (now 8s. 6d. in the £). People who sign a Covenant but who are only paying tax at a reduced rate may be liable for extra tax, calculated on the gross amount of the Covenant, at the difference between the reduced rate and the standard rate. In many cases it is still advantageous from the PCC's point of view to accept Deeds of Covenant from persons not paying Income Tax at the full standard rate, a reduction being made in the amount covenanted compensates if any extra tax is suffered. This does not necessarily involve parish officials in knowing the private tax status of covenanters. Such Covenants should, however, only be accepted by parish treasurers who are fully competent to make and explain these necessary adjustments. It is not always easy to operate the Covenant scheme in a parish, but it is worth the effort of every PCC to consider the possibilities. In most cases it will lead to a large increase in parish finances, often at no extra cost, and with comparatively little organization.

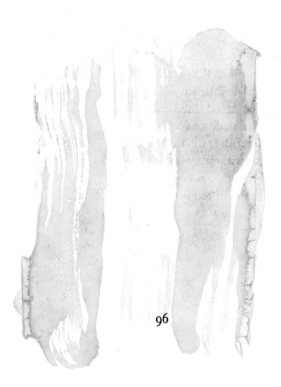